THE MARTYRS OF CASTELFIDARDO

MARQUIS DE SÉGUR

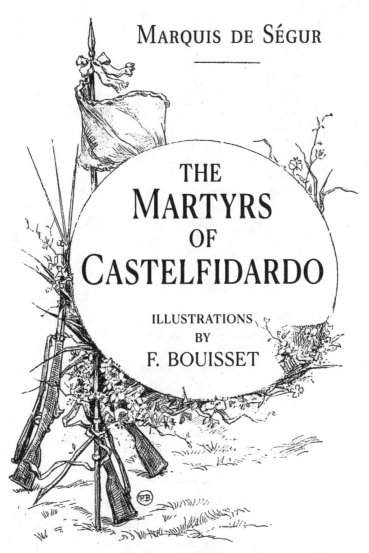

THE
MARTYRS
OF
CASTELFIDARDO

ILLUSTRATIONS
BY
F. BOUISSET

TRANSLATED FROM FRENCH BY A MEMBER OF
THE PRESENTATION CONVENT, CO. KERRY, IRELAND.

EDITED BY BRENDAN CASSELL

AROUCA
PRESS

ISBN: 978-1-990685-95-8 (pbk)
ISBN: 978-1-990685-96-5 (hc)

Arouca Press
PO Box 55003
Bridgeport PO
Waterloo, ON N2J 0A5
Canada
www.aroucapress.com
Send inquiries to info@aroucapress.com

Cover Image: The Martyrdom of Joseph-
Louis Guerin and the Papal Zouavesat the
battle of Castelfidardo, source unknown.

CONTENTS

Founded in 2023, PAPAL ZOUAVE INTERNATIONAL is an organization dedicated to promoting and preserving the memory of the Papal Zouaves, a unit of brave Catholic soldiers that came from across Christendom to defend the Papal States and Bl. Pope Pius IX during the 9th Crusade between 1860–1870.

To learn more visit papalzouave.com

Monseigneur de Mérode.

EDITOR'S PREFACE

GENERAL HISTORY OF THE PAPAL ZOUAVES

HE VIOLENT FALL OF THE PAPAL STATES and the unification of Italy is a much-overlooked period of history. Even more overlooked are the brave Papal Soldiers who sacrificed their lives for the cause of the Church. The following preface will give a summarized account of the events between 1859–1870 so the reader will have a fuller appreciation of this book.

There was a time when the Pope ruled over most of central Italy. Given by Pepin the Short in 754, the Pope's temporal power was called the Papal States. For over 1000 years the Papal States helped secure the sovereignty of the Church, while at times contested and not always sufficient to prevent temporal interference into the affairs of the Church. Nonetheless, the Papal States served as an effective bulwark of the City of God against the City of Man. Without a temporal power, the Pope and the Church would be subjected greatly to the affairs of the City of Man. Imagine the persecution the Church would have faced if they didn't have the Leonine city to defend themselves from the Revolutionary French, Nationalist Italians, and Nazi Germany.

In the mid-19th century, Italy was divided into 10 different territories. In Southern Italy was the Kingdom of the Two Sicilies (its last ruler and his mother are both on the path to sainthood, Servant of God Francis II and Blessed Maria of Savoy). In Central Italy the Papal States (the last "Pope-King" is also on the path to sainthood, Blessed Pope Pius IX) and San Marino. In Northern Italy was the Kingdom of Sardinia-Piedmont and Monaco, along with Austrian controlled Kingdom of Lombardy and Venetia and the Austrian influenced Duchies of Parma, Tuscany, and Modena.

This time period saw the rise of nationalism, and many revolutionaries on the peninsula got caught up in nationalistic fervor. With the help of secret societies, individuals such as Cavour, Garibaldi, Mazzini, and Victor Emmanuel II, despite conflicting desires for particular styles of government, wanted nothing more than a united Italy, even if it was achieved through violence, conniving, and treachery. The Church and the Pope were about to suffer greatly.

Everything came to a head in 1859. The King of Sardinia-Piedmont, Victor Emmanuel II, and his Prime Minister Cavour began their campaign to unite Italy. A secret agreement was signed between Cavour and French Emperor Napoleon III early in the year, and the Emperor promised to help push the Austrians out of the peninsula in return for Savoy and Nice near the French border. In March the Piedmontese began mobilizing along the border with Lombardy provoking Austria to mobilize themselves. In April, when the Kingdom of Sardinia refused to de-mobilize, Austria invaded. France quickly joined Piedmont, and together after several months Austria was defeated.

During this time, Sardinia staged uprisings in Tuscany, Parma, Modena, and the northernmost territory of the Papal States, the Romagna, causing them to destabilize. Shortly after the war ended, these territories were annexed by Sardinia-Piedmont. With Austria defeated, they ceded Lombardy to France, who gave it to Sardinia, and in turn Sardinia ceded Savoy and Nice to France. Napoleon III tried his best to influence Bl. Pius IX to accept the annexation of the Romanga to Sardinia-Piedmont. However, the Holy Father held his ground and excommunicated all of those who had taken part in its capture. Now was the time to resist.

There were two options in front of Bl. Pius IX. The Cardinal Secretary of State Giacomo Antonelli wanted to rely on diplomacy while Monsignor Xavier de Mérode, a private chamberlain of the Pope, believed that diplomacy could not be relied upon, as it was not enough to curb the nationalistic fervor of King Victor Emmanuel II and the Italian revolutionaries. He believed the only way to defend the temporal power was by force, and strengthening the Papal Army would be necessary to protect the Papal States.

This would be a huge undertaking as the Papal Army was very weak and ill equipped. However, Mérode had a vision that the Army could be revitalized through a multinational force of pious Catholics from around the world akin to a Crusade.

Bl. Pius IX was convinced, he approved of Mérode's plan, and promoted him to the Papal Minister of Arms. The volunteers of the Pope would go on to view themselves as soldiers fighting in the 9th Crusade.

The plan was put into effect immediately, with more than 5,000 foreign recruits being raised from almost 30 different countries. Most were Irish, Austrian, French, and Dutch. The Austrians formed 5 Battalions of light infantry: the Irish formed the Battalion of St. Patrick, and the French and Dutch formed the Franco-Belgian Battalion. Here is the beginning of the Papal Zouaves; after the 1860 campaign, the Franco-Belgians transitioned into the Papal Zouaves.

Many of these volunteers came from noble lineage. Additionally, many had ancestors or relatives that had fought in other Counter-Revolutionary efforts such as the war in the Vendée. In fact, the first group of foreign volunteers was the Crusaders of Cathelineau, led by Henri de Cathelineau, the grandson of Vendéen General Jacques Cathelineau. The group existed only a few months before being incorporated into the Franco-Belgian Battalion.

Former French General de la Moricière was selected to lead the Papal Army. Motivated by his Catholic faith, he understood how important the coming conflict would be. In an address given to new volunteers on Easter Sunday 1860, he said:

> At the sound of the grand voice which lately apprised the world from the Vatican of the dangers threatening the patrimony of St. Peter, Catholics were moved, and their emotion soon spread to every part of the earth. This is because Christianity is not merely the religion of the civilized world, but the animating principle of civilization; it is because the Papacy is the keystone of the arch of Christianity, and all Christian nations seem, in these days, to be conscious of those great varieties which are our faith. The revolution today threatens Europe as Islamism did of old, and now, as then, the cause of the Pope is that of civilization and liberty throughout the world. Soldiers, have confidence, and believe that God will raise our courage to the level of the great cause whose defense He has entrusted to our arms.

La Moricière was also important because he wanted a unit of Zouaves in his army. Knowing firsthand how effective the type of light infantry unit was, as he led a regiment of Zouaves in Algeria in 1838. The origins of the Zouaves can be traced back to 1831. After the French conquest of Algeria, they made allies with the Kaybles, a Berber people living in the mountains. One of their tribes, the Zwawa were known as fierce warriors, and they wanted to fight under their new rulers. Battalions of these native Zwawa were formed under the name Zouave. Shortly thereafter, companies of French Zouaves began to form. This type of elite light infantry unit became extremely popular in the 19th century with units being raised in the Union, the Confederacy, Poland, Spain, and of course the Papal States. At the time the Franco-Belgian battalion was a Zouave unit in all but name and it wasn't long before their commander Major Becdelievre pushed for the adoption of the Zouave uniform.

In front of the Basilica of St. John Lateran each of the new Papal Army recruits made the following oath: "I swear to Almighty God to be obedient and faithful to my sovereign, the Roman Pontiff, Our very Holy Father Pope Pius IX, and to his legitimate successors. I swear to serve with honor and fidelity and to sacrifice my life for the defense of his august and sacred person, for the maintenance of his sovereignty and for the maintenance of his rights." Many of those who swore that oath did indeed follow it unto their deaths.

Seeking to continue uniting the Peninsula, Cavour secretly coordinated with Garibaldi for his Red Shirts to seize the Kingdom of the Two Sicilies. By May, his forces had landed in Sicily, and Garibaldi declared himself dictator in the name of Victor Emmanuel II. By September, the entire Kingdom was under his control with the exception of over ten thousand holdouts in Capua, Civitella del Tronto, and Gaeta commanded by Francis II. All eyes were now on the Papal States.

A French garrison was stationed in Rome which was supposed to help guarantee the Pope's temporal power. However, Cavour had received Napoleon III's blessing to take all of the Papal States with the exception of the Lazio region (Rome and its surrounding territory) without his interference. With this act Napoleon III turned his back on his Catholic subjects.

In early September Sardinia and the secret societies began inciting civil unrest in the northern territories of the Papal States. Under the guise of restoring order, Sardinia invaded the Papal States with 38,000–70,000 soldiers on September 11, 1860. The only hope the Papal States had in winning was if Austria sent troops to reinforce the Papal Army through the port of Ancona in the N. E. of the Papal States. In anticipation of these supposed reinforcements, the Papal plan was to have the majority of the Army maneuver to the city and defend it from siege.

Unfortunately, the majority of the Army was routed during the Battle of Castelfidardo on September 18, 1860. The loss was so catastrophic that it came to be known as a massacre and the fallen Papal Soldiers, as martyrs. The field was filled with so many noble Catholic youth of France that an Italian General commented, "You would think this was a list of invites for a ball given by Louis XIV!" On September 29, Ancona fell and with it the majority of the Papal States. The Pope's temporal power was reduced to only the Lazio region, which included Rome. Bl. Pius IX protested these losses; however, the majority of the world ignored him. While for the moment, the fighting stopped, the threat against the Papal States continued. The revolutionaries would not stop until all of Italy was united.

Over the next few years, the Papal Army grew and became more well-trained. The Franco-Belgian Battalion officially transitioned to the Papal Zouaves on January 1, 1861. Over a week later, on January 10, 1861 the Papal Zouave battalion went to St. John Lateran to swear a solemn oath to defend the Papal States. The Papal Zouave Chaplain, Father Daniel, administered the oath to them. He said:

> So far you have committed yourself individually but today all together we want to solemnly swear fidelity to God, to His service, to the Church and her rights. To its kingly head, temporal prince, spiritual head, we promise to defend his rights and die rather than abandon them cowardly. For my part, gentleman, in the presence of this battalion which I respect and love in the presence of God and the Church, I swear to remain always faithful to the Church, to her doctrine,

and to her rights. I say this oath out of complete fidelity and devotion to serve you and for the salvation of your souls. Now I will hear your oath."

The Papal Zouaves then proceeded to say their solemn oath.

I swear to Almighty God to be obedient and faithful to my sovereign, the Roman Pontiff, our very Holy Father, Pope Pius IX, and his legitimate successors. I swear to serve him with honor and fidelity and to sacrifice my life for the defense of his august and sacred person, for the support of his sovereignty and for the maintenance of his rights. I swear not to belong to any civil or religious sect, to any secret society or corporation, whatever they might be, having for its direct or indirect goal to offend the Catholic religion and to corrupt society. I swear to not join any sect or society condemned by the decrees of the Roman Pontiffs. I swear also to the very good and great God to not have any direct or indirect communication with the enemies, whoever they might be, of religion and the Roman Pontiffs. I swear all of this on the holy Gospel, so help me God. Through our Lord Jesus Christ, Amen." Immediately after the oath was said the Officers raised their swords and arms were presented by the battalion. Thus, the Church had new protectors.

The author of this book will occasionally use Franco-Belgian and Papal Zouave interchangeably, because the Papal Zouaves viewed the Franco-Belgians as part of their pedigree and as such truly considered them part of their unit. Over 10,000 men would join the Papal Zouaves over the course of its lifetime. The largest the unit ever got was in 1868, a full regiment with 4 battalions, totaling almost 5,000 men.

However, they started off as a 600-man Battalion with six companies.

Unfortunately, due to a disagreement between Merode, Becdelievre resigned command of the unit in March. Most of the soldiers wanted the Athanse de Charette, the Great-Nephew of Vendean General François de Charette to lead the Unit. However, since he was a legitimist, Bl. Pius IX didn't want to anger Napoleon III and risk losing the French garrison stationed in

Rome. Instead, Swiss Colonel Allet, who had been in the Papal Army for many years was chosen to lead the unit and Charette was promoted to Major. His time would come however, as he would eventually lead a contingent of French Papal Zouaves during the Franco-Prussian War, and in a sense, he was a father figure among the Papal Zouaves.

Over the next few years, the Papal Zouaves lived mostly a Garrison life. The main threat the Papal States faced was brigands and other criminals along the border and in the mountains. There was an occasional border dispute with the Piedmontese. The largest occurred on August 4, 1862, when 400 Piedmontese soldiers encroached over the Southern Papal States border and harassed the town of Ceprano which had many Neapolitan refugees from the Kingdom of Two Sicilies. Two companies of Piedmontese attempted to ford a river to get into the town when a platoon of 17 Papal Zouaves commanded by Lt. Mousty engaged them, successfully repelling the assault. The Piedmontese retreated in great disorder, leaving 5 dead and 25 wounded. There were no injuries among the Papal Zouaves. The Victory at Ceprano showed the Piedmontese that the Papal States were serious about their borders.

Among other things, the Papal Zouaves were used in many religious ceremonies such as processions, masses on feast days, and whenever Bl. Pius IX spoke from his balcony. The unit was defined by their piety and devotion to their faith. In order to become a Papal Zouave, a letter of recommendation had to be obtained from a priest. All recruits had to start out as a private regardless of social class, which even included many nobility who joined the unit, such as Prince Alfonso Carlso de Bourbon the future rightful King of Spain. Pay and rations were also very poor, a half penny a day, soup, bread, and coffee. Despite the low pay many were very generous with their tithing. Most of their free time was spent inside of Churches in prayer or in various Catholic confraternities.

However, the monotony of Garrison life did not suit everyone. After an initial boost in numbers from emboldened recruits due to the loss in 1860, numbers began to drop. This occurred in other units as well; after 1860, the Battalion of St. Patrick was turned into the Company of St. Patrick, and they were ultimately dissolved, with the remainder of the soldiers being incorporated into the Papal Zouaves in 1862. By 1863 the number of Papal Zouaves dropped to 300. However, this would soon change.

It started with another backstab from Napoleon III. On September 15, 1864 France signed an agreement with Italy known as the September Convention. It was agreed that Napoleon III would evacuate the French garrison in Rome over the next two years. Additionally, Italy, among other things, promised not to attack the Pope's territory. However, this agreement was merely for show, as it opened the door for Garibaldi and his Red Shirts to invade and cede Rome to Italy without French interference just as they did with the Kingdom of Two Sicilies in 1860. If they failed, Victor Emmanuel II could pretend that they had nothing to do with Garibaldi.

When the agreement was made public in early 1865, there was outrage in Rome at the betrayal of Napoleon III, as it foreshadowed events to come. Upon hearing the news, General de la Moricière, who had been living in France since the defeat of the Papal Army in 1860, prepared to return to lead the army. However, he died and General Herman Kanzler was made Commander of the Papal Army; in 1860 Monsignor Merode resigned as pro-minister of arms, and Kanzler also assumed that position.

There was a surge of Papal Zouave recruits as the threat to the Papal States grew significantly. The unit grew to 1500 men, two more line companies and a depot company were added. Activity with revolutionaries and brigands also increased during this time as they attempted to capitalize off the French exit.

Recruitment swelled again in 1866 after Piedmont passed a series of anti-clerical laws which included imprisonment of bishops, banning of Papal encyclicals, forbidding religious processions, closing of seminaries, subjecting priests to conscription, among many more heinous and anti-catholic acts.

Meanwhile, in the summer of 1866, Victor Emmaneul II joined forces with Prussia against the Austrians in the Seven Weeks' War. The goal of the Kingdom of Italy was to remove the last vestige of Austrian influence on the peninsula. While Italy did not fare so well during the war, Prussia was victorious and the Austrian controlled Kingdom of Venetia was ceded to France who then ceded the territory to Italy, just like what happened with Nice and Savoy in 1860. By December 1866 the French Garrison had left Rome. All that remained between Victor Emmanuel II and a united Italy was Bl. Pius IX and the last remaining territory of the Papal States.

By January 1867, the Papal Zouaves had swelled to a regiment with 4 battalions. Confident in God and His soldiers, Bl. Pius IX announced the convening of the first Vatican Council in October 1869. While the enemies of the Church were plotting to attack the Papal States, a terrible cholera outbreak erupted in the region, hitting the town of Albano just outside of Rome particularly hard. The civil government in the town collapsed, the mayor and most of the residents fled leaving piles of bodies in the street and the sick to fend for themselves. The only figures that stayed and helped the Sisters of Charity in their care for the sick was the archbishop, Cardinal Altieri, and the vacationing and exiled royal family of the Two Sicilies. The disease would claim the archbishop and the queen mother.

Help arrived in the form of the 6th company of the 2nd battalion of Papal Zouaves. The Lieutenant in charge of the first detachment of Zouaves that arrived was the first to pick up a corpse and carry it to the cemetery. He called out to his men: "I set the example; those who want to work with me stay here, those who don't feel up to it go back to the barracks." The Papal Zouaves followed his example at their own peril. By August 20 the epidemic had subsided but not before claiming two Dutchmen in the unit. One of them, Henri Peters, found consolation in his final moments by holding a crucifix. With his dying lips he kissed it fervently, and exclaimed, "I know that Heaven is before me when all this is past."

With the summer epidemic over, the French garrison no longer in Rome, and Lombardy under Italian control, Victor Emmanul II initiated his plans to capture Rome. The prime minister at the time, Rattazzi and his cabinet, supplied Garibaldi with arms, supplies, and money and allowed him to raise an army. In late September, Garibaldi and his two sons began their invasion of the Lazio region. Their goal was to cause civil unrest and seize Rome, and they hoped that their invasion would cause revolutionaries to rise up and assist them in their takeover, much like what happened in 1849 when revolutionaries seized Rome and forced Bl. Pius IX into exile. He was restored less than a year later with the assistance of France, Spain, and the Two Sicilies. If Garibaldi failed to take Rome the plan was to have the Kingdom of Italy declare that due to the civil unrest, they needed to send their Army to "restore order."

The Red Shirts numbered well over 10,000 while the Papal Army numbered around 13,000, but had an effective fighting force only around 8,000 with over 2,000 Papal Zouaves. Over the next month the Papal Army fought bravely and fended off most attacks that came from the Garibaldians. In late October, the Red Shirts attempted to incite a revolution in Rome, but it failed to gain any traction. On October 22 about 500 Red Shirts infiltrated the city and bombed over a dozen places. One of them was a Papal Zouave barracks at the Palazzo Serritorsi. The explosion destroyed the building and killed 25 Zouaves, most of them from the band and four civilians, including a little girl. The attacks that night from the Red Shirts were repelled by the Papal Zouaves. More attacks occurred the following day, but they too failed. The city clearly was not going to fall to the revolutionary force.

During this time, Empress Eugenie and pressure from French Catholics convinced Napoleon III to denounce the invasion of the Pope's territory and to send him a sizable force to help defeat the Red Shirts. Garibaldi attempted to seize Rome before the French force arrived, but he was unable to do so.

On October 30, the French force arrived in Rome. Garibaldi, hoping to draw France into a conflict with the Kingdom of Italy, pulled his forces back in an attempt to link up with the Italian Royal Army. Realizing his plan, the commander of the Papal Army General Kanzler, with French reinforcements, pursued the Red Shirts and routed them in the town of Mentana on November 3, 1867. The Papal Zouaves were the tip of the spear during the battle, and it was through their efforts that the battle was won. By nightfall, the Papal Army had Garibaldi's Army trapped and surrounded inside the town. The next morning the Red Shirts surrendered, and the Papal and French forces occupied the town. Unfortunately, Garibaldi escaped capture.

He had slipped away during the battle with half his force into the safety of Italian territory. Not wanting to start a war they were unprepared for, the Royal Army did not assist the Red Shirts. Garibaldi himself would never again invade the Papal States. The victory at Mentana is considered the greatest battle ever won by the Papal Zouaves. A monument was dedicated to their victory and to the fallen at the Campo Verano cemetery in Rome. The victory at Mentana bought the Papal States three more years. Which in turn allowed the First Vatican Council to happen starting on December 8, 1869. Without the heroism of the Papal Zouaves, would the dogma of papal infallibility and other fruits of the Council have been promulgated?

The victory at Mentna led to another surge in recruitment with the unit reaching its highest numbers in 1868, almost 5,000 soldiers. Over the next three years things were relatively quiet. That was, until the start of the Franco-Prussian War in the summer of 1870. After the Battle of Mentana, Napoleon III kept a garrison of 4,000 soldiers in Rome. However, his war with Prussia was not going well, and he was getting desperate. He recalled the force in Rome and declared he was returning to the rules of the September convention. On September 2, Napoleon III was captured after his defeat at the Battle of Sedan. With France out of the way and Austria too weak to assist the Papal States, Victor Emmanuel II pounced on the opportunity. Afraid of having Garibaldi invade and risk destabilizing his monarchy, Victor Emmanuel II decided to use his Royal Army to invade Rome.

On September 9, the Royal Army was posed on the Lazio region border. Victor Emmanuel II wrote Bl. Pope Pius IX a letter and sent Count Gustavo Ponza di San Martino to deliver it the following day on September 10. The letter, which really was just a guise to request a bloodless takeover, claimed that due to the removal of French troops from the city, it was necessary for his forces to occupy the Eternal City so that they could maintain law and order from Roman revolutionaries. A strange thing to say since there were no revolutionary uprisings in Rome at the time. Bl. Pius IX did not appreciate the hypocrisy in the letter. He replied to Count Ponza. "What a race of vipers! Whited sepulchers! and wanting in faith!" Count

Ponza became so afraid that he rushed out of the room and mistook a window for a door, almost falling to his death. Bl. Pius IX refused to be bullied. He rejected Victor Emmanuel II's offer, an action which certainly would lead to war, one which would be very difficult. The Italian Army had over 75,000 troops stationed on the frontier ready to invade the last of the Papal States, meanwhile the Papal Army had only around 12,000 men. General Kanzler believed that as long as he kept the Italian divisions divided, he could launch a successful offensive strike. However, an offensive attack required approval from the Pope. Kanzler met with Bl. Pius IX immediately after his meeting with Count Ponza.

The Pope disappointed the Papal Army, and he rejected any offensive operations as he believed the war could not be won. His orders were that, upon invasion, all elements of the Papal Army were to fall back on Rome and wait for the arrival of the Italians, with the exception of the Papal port of Civita Vecchia, so that the Pope could have a potential route to escape if needed. Bits of resistance on the way to Rome were allowed to show the world that Italy was unjustly usurping the temporal power of the Pope by force, additionally a defense of the Holy City was allowed to a point. The invasion began on September 11th, the Papal forces began to fall back to Rome.

Bits of fighting and heroism were done on the way; a few days later over 8,500 Papal Soldiers were inside the city ready to lay down their lives for their Pontiff. By September 18, the city was surrounded by over 40,000 Italian soldiers, including a large contingent of Red Shirts who came to wreak havoc on the city. Wanting to avoid further bloodshed and believing that a sufficient show of force had been displayed Bl. Pius IX ordered a "surrender at first cannon shot." General Kanzler petitioned the Pope to allow a greater defense to preserve the honor of his army. Bl. Pius IX was swayed and allowed a defense until "a breach has been opened" in the walls.

The Italian attack on Rome began in the early morning hours on September 20. The Papal Army put up a valiant resistance, taking "a breach in the walls" as loosely as possible. After several hours it became clear that a breach had been made. At 10:00 am Bl. Pius IX ordered the white flag to be flown over St. Peter's Basilica. He turned to the diplomats with him and said "Sirs, I give the order to surrender. Abandoned by all, I had to succumb sooner or later. I must not shed blood uselessly. You are my witnesses, Sirs, that the foreigner enters here only by force."

As the Papal Soldiers marched back to the Vatican to await further instruction, anticlerical and secret society members accosted and even attacked the Papal Soldiers. Over the coming days, some were even murdered, and several churches and convents ransacked and destroyed. The Papal Army spent the night bivouacked in St. Peter's Square. The following morning before the military was disbanded and everyone sent home, the Papal Army had one last formation and a final blessing was given by Bl. Pope Pius IX.

An Irish Papal Zouave, Patrick Keyes O'Clery gave this account of the emotional scene:

> When all the soldiers were lined up, facing the Vatican and ready to leave, Colonel Allet stepped forward and, his voice broken with emotion, shouted: "Mes enfants! Vive Pie Neuf!" A mighty cheer broke out from the troops. Just at that moment the Pope appeared on the balcony, and, raising his hands to heaven, prayed: "May God bless my faithful children!" The enthusiasm of that supreme moment was indescribable. With a frantic Eljen! (Hurrah) a Hungarian Zouave drew his sword, and immediately, with a simultaneous scuff of steel, thousands of unsheathed swords glinted in the sun. The scene was absolutely moving. At the thought of leaving the Holy Father, tears of bitter regret ran down the cheeks of those men who had defied death in so many desperate battles. The trumpets gave the order to advance and, as it moved, the head of the column let out a last sad cry of "Long live Pius IX!" which, echoed row after row, was repeated by the whole army and by the crowd gathered to watch the departure.

The Papal Zouaves were put on a train and sent to Civita Vecchia. Under horrid conditions and lack of food they awaited to board steamers to return home. Thus the thousand year reign of the Papal States was over. The final composition of the regiment truly reflects the international makeup of the Papal Zouaves. The unit consisted of the following nationalities after Rome fell on September 20, 1870. 1,172 Dutch, 760 French, 563 Belgians, 297 Canadians, British, and Irish, 242 Italians from various states on the Peninsula, 113 Germans, 37 Spaniards, 19 Swiss, 15 Austrians, 7 Russians and Poles, 5 Americans, 4 Portuguese, 2 Brazilians, 2 Ecuadorian, 1 Peruvian, 1 Greek, 1 Monacan, 1 Chilean, 1 Ottoman Turk, and 1 Chinese. Not included were some nationalities who had finished service contracts with the unit and either failed to return to Rome before September 20 or had moved onto other things. These include but are not limited to Papal Zouaves from the Maltese, South Sea Islands, India, Africa, Mexico, and Circassia.

Having achieved victory, the new United Kingdom of Italy applied its anti-clerical laws of 1866 to Rome. Bl. Pius IX refused to acknowledge the takeover as legitimate. He considered himself a prisoner in the Vatican and refused to step outside its walls for the rest of his life. General Kanzler in solidarity adopted this same position in solidarity. He retained his title as Minister of War honorarily. Subsequent popes remained as prisoners in the Vatican until the Lateran treaty in 1929 between Pope Pius XI and Mussolini, which formalized the relationship between Italy and the Vatican.

For most of the Papal Zouaves, the fight was over. However, the majority of the French Papal Zouaves continued fighting with the unit as they reorganized under the new name the Volunteers of the West. The Volunteers fought to defend France during the remainder of the Franco-Prussian war. They are most well known for their bravery at the battle of Loigny Patay. On December 2, 1870 General de Sonis and Colonel de Charette led the unit in a 300-man charge against the Bavarians. They initially had the upper hand; however, no other French forces came to reinforce them. Upon realizing their true number, the Bavarians pushed them back. Out of the 300 in the charge, 218 died. Their flag had the image of the Sacred Heart of Jesus with the words, "Heart of Jesus save France." After the war the unit was disbanded. Additionally, in 1873, many Papal Zouave veterans joined the Carlist Zouave Battalion under former Papal Zouave Prince Alfonso de Bourbon during the Third

Carlist War. Many of the Papal Zouaves held onto hope that one day they would put on their uniform again and retake the Holy City for their beloved Pope. Unfortunately, these events never came to pass. The Papal Zouaves continued their fight against the Revolution in other ways. Such as through missionary efforts, writing in Catholic publications, participating in government, and starting Catholic businesses.

OVERVIEW OF THE BATTLE OF CASTELFIDARDO

Now that a general understanding of the history of the Papal Zouaves has been established, we will return to the battle that this work is centered on and take a deeper look on the happenings of September 18, 1860, and the events that preceded it.

The Kingdom of Sardinia-Piedmont invaded the Papal States with over 70,000 soldiers on September 11, 1860 under the guise of restoring order in the region due to civil unrest. The reality of the situation was they had caused the unrest themselves in order to come up with an excuse to invade the Papal States.

The only hope that Bl. Pope Pius IX had in beating back the Piedmontese was if Austria or another Catholic power sent troops to reinforce the Papal Army through the port at Ancona in the North Eastern part of the Papal States. In anticipation of these supposed reinforcements, the papal plan was to have the majority of the Army move to the city and defend it from siege.

Making his way to Ancona with a sizable force, on September 16, the Commander of the Papal Army, General de la Moricière, arrived in Loreto, a town which was just 20 miles south of Ancona and contained the Holy House of Loreto (Believed to be the home of Jesus, Mary, and Joseph. Angels carried the home to Loreto sometime in the middle-ages). The town was occupied by a squadron of lancers who were quickly dispelled by the Pontificals.

From there he determined that the Italian IV Corps, which consisted of almost 16,500 men had set up a defensive line around the adjacent town of Castelfidardo, which was directly on his route to Ancona. Indeed, General Caldini of the IV Corps had set up a 10 kilometer front extending from Osimo to Castelfidardo blocking the Papal Army's path to Ancona. Going around wasn't an option for La Moricière option as the

Italian V Corps was on his tail. He determined the best course of action was to push through the IV corps at Castelfidardo.

That night, a four-person reconnaissance party was sent out by General de la Morcière to assess the situation along the road to Ancona. About 30 yards from the road they identified Piedmontese artillery, which opened fire mortally wounding Mizael Mesre de Pas of the Guides of La Morcière. He became the first casualty of the battle.

The following day, a brigade led by Colonel Pimodan, which was following the rear of La Morcière's forces arrived in Loreto, after marching 106 miles over several days with little rest. While the senior officers planned the battle the men prepared themselves for a fight. Colonel Becdelievre, the Commander of the Franco-Belgian Battalion said to his men

> Tomorrow, at this hour, several among us will have appeared before God. Now, you know that a man should be clean when he appears before Him. Let those who are not so go around to the chaplain.

I have just left him myself the men received Holy Communion the morning of the 17 and 18. After consulting local inhabitants, La Morcière found out that Caldini had not effectively covered a secondary road that led to Ancona, believing that the Musone river (a river that separated Loreto and Castelfidardo) was too deep at that point making it unfordable. However, it was fordable and a plan was conceived to cross it.

General de la Morcière's plan was a fix and bypass mission. He split his 6,800-man force into three columns: two would attempt to hold the enemy in place and slow down their advance, by occupying the high ground on the opposite side of the Musone, allowing one column to maneuver around the enemy without engaging them. They would cross the Musone river at three separate points. The left column, the first fixing force, commanded by Colonel Pimodan would ford the right bank of the river and reach a collection of buildings known as Casa Andreani-Catena the "Lower Farm" From there he would wheel left to the face the Italians left flank. Engaging them he would continue uphill a few hundred meters to Casa Serenella del Mira the "Upper Farm" and from there move to the summit of the hill where there was a third set of buildings. This would allow him to fix any Piedmontese forces from attacking the Papal left flank. This fight would be difficult as large amounts of Piedmontese Bersaglieri occupied the farms and woodlines in addition to artillery batteries along the slopes.

The center column led by General de la Moricière, would ford the river a few hundred meters downstream from Pimodan then wheel left and establish a reserve line for the first column. The right column, which was made up primarily of the baggage train, reserve artillery, and gendarmes, would cross the river further downstream and bypass the enemy to make their way onto the road and head directly for Ancona. After they made it on the road, the center column would follow after them with Pimodan's left column continuing to cover their movements, until all of their forces were across the river on their way to Ancona.

The main objective of the battle wasn't the defeat of the enemy but rather the fixing of Italian troops so that the majority of the Papal forces could bypass and make their way to Ancona.

A French priest described the scene of the morning of the 18th just before the Army set out:

> The scene worthy of the epoch of the Crusades, and which as a priest and a Frenchman, gave me the greatest consolation. At 4 o'clock Moriciere, Pimodan, and all the staff-officers, the guides, and the German regiments, the foreigns and natives, all received Holy Communion.
>
> I saw the greater number of them prostrate in prayer… On the ramparts, towards the north side of the plain, perceiving a movement amongst the enemy's troops, which seemed like a swarm of ants in the distance, the Franco-Belgians said to me:
>
> "Bless me, Monsieur l'Abbe, for we shall never meet again on earth."

At 8:30 am the 3,500-man left column commanded by Pimodan set off. It consisted of 5 battalions of infantry (Including a large contingent from the Franco-Belgian Battalion), 12 pieces of artillery protected by a Company from St Patrick's

Battalion, and two squadrons of cavalry. A flag that was flown at the Battle of Lepanto was removed from the Holy House and was carried ahead of the Papal forces. Thirty minutes later the 3,300-man center column commanded by La Moricière followed. It consisted of four infantry battalions, a detachment of cavalry, a half squadron of mounted gendarmes, and some artillery. The orders for leaving weren't communicated well so most of the men left without eating breakfast.

The Italians were caught by surprise. They had poor intelligence and did not expect a fight on the 18th, nor did they believe the river by the left flank was fordable. The first shots of the battle started at 9:20 am when the Swiss and Franco-Belgians in the lead column engaged with a company of Bersaglieri defending the riverbank and the lower farm. The elements along the river bank became displaced, scattered among the reeds but continued firing on the advancing Papal Army.

The Italians sent three companies of Bersaglieri from the Upper Farm to reinforce and counter-attack, at the same time another company from a nearby position heard the fighting and rushed to engage, fierce hand to hand fighting broke out between the reinforcements of the lead elements of Pimodan's column. The Irish company that was in charge of moving artillery pieces was targeted while crossing the river, but managed to stave off the attack and kill a Bersaglieri officer. Overwhelmed, the Piedmontese withdrew to the lower and then the Upper Farm. There was a temporary halt in the Papal advance when the Swiss Foreign Carabineers were accidently fired upon by the 2nd Indigenous Cacciatori (an infantry unit consisting of local Romans). However, no fratricide resulted from the incident. The commander was relieved of duty and replaced on the spot by General Pimodan, the advanced continued immediately afterwards.

The Franco-Belgians fixed bayonets and charged toward the Lower Farm buildings, occupying them and seizing 100 prisoners. By 10:30 am the Swiss and the Franco-Belgians had secured the Lower Farm. With his whole column now across the river General Pimodan re-grouped his forces. He set his artillery and established an assault line and reserve line. Meanwhile, the Italians sent an infantry regiment to reinforce the struggling

Bersaglieri. Pimodan wanted to keep up the fast-paced tempo of the advance. After the lower farm was secured, He gave his troops only a few minutes rest while they reorganized and started their attack uphill towards the Upper Farm, General Pimodan personally took command of this charge. The Upper Farm was only a few hundred meters away but the charge was very dangerous. The terrain was open and they were completely exposed to fire from the Piedmontese hiding behind the Upper Farms walls. It was most likely during this advance, that Joseph Louis Guerin, the Papal Zouave who has come closest to Sainthood, received a mortal wound in his chest. Pimodan and his forces under a hail of balls reached the Upper Farm, hand to hand fighting once again broke out.

Thanks to the bravery of Captain Charrette (Future Papal Zouave Battalion Commander and General of the Volunteers of the West) and the Franco-Belgian Battalion, the Bersaglieri retreated from the Upper Farm to the top of the hill. However, the Pontificals could not rest for long. There was a small house at the summit of the hill, they needed to seize this piece of key terrain before the Piedmontese reinforcements arrived so they could successfully repel any quick reaction forces and allow the baggage train to bypass to Ancona.

The mission hindered on this very moment. Around 10:50 am, despite fatigue from fighting for an hour and a half straight and from hunger after not eating breakfast, they charged to the summit.

As the Pontificals were about the reach the top, two battalions of Italian reinforcements that were called up earlier arrived and poured over the crest of the hill. This stopped the Papal Advance in their tracks, Pimodan on horseback rallied his troops, ordering them to continue charging and counter-attack.

During this counter-attack, Captain Charette encountered one of his former classmates from the L'Academie Militaire de Turin, Captain Tromboni, now in the Royal Army of Piedmont and leading a company of Bersaglieri against the Pontifical troops. Charette upon encountering Tromboni exclaimed "En garde!" and called to his troops to stand fast. Soldiers from both sides briefly lowered their weapons and stopped fighting to witness a chivalric Sabre duel between former classmates.

Tromboni was bested and fell bleeding profusely. Charette declared "This man is my prisoner. Take him to an ambulance and care for him." He then turned to his company and in a loud and commanding voice bid his soldiers to advance "En avant, les efants!", and the battle then resumed.

The Pontificals briefly regained their momentum and were only meters from their goal when the remaining reinforcements from the Piedmontese regiment arrived. Gaining numerical superiority and having the advantage of fighting downhill they overwhelmed the Papal forces, sending them back toward the Upper Farm which was now on fire.

While attempting to rally his men once again, General Pimodan was shot three times. In the jaw, then foot, and finally his chest. Each time he was struck he shouted "Courage, my children, God is with us!" He fell from his horse and was taken back to the Lower Farm. As more Italian reinforcements poured over the hill the Papal troops lost their momentum. They retreated back to the Upper Farm, which was now on fire.

Meanwhile, around noon, La Moricière's column had successfully forded the river, he was having trouble making out what was happening on the hill so he rode with a few staff officers to the Lower Farm to investigate. There he saw Pimodan on a stretcher pleading to be given the honor of dying on the battlefield instead of an aid station.

This sight, the unwillingness to abandon his comrades, along with the belief that the battle could be won made La Moricière abandon his original plan of getting as many soldiers to escape to Ancona as possible. Instead, he wanted a total victory. He ordered his column to the Lower Farm and the remainder of Pimodan's reserve line to reinforce the Upper Farm.

As the center column moved to the Lower Farm, they took fire from Piedmontese artillery. The 1st Foreign Infantry Regiment panicked, threw down their arms, and ran. This panic quickly spread to the other units of the center column and most fled. Within minutes and without firing a shot the central column collapsed.

The panic then spread to the reserve echelon of Pimodan's column enroute to reinforce the Upper Farm. The 2nd Cacciatori Battalion upon seeing the intense fighting at the farm, turned and ran, with exception of the Guides of General de la Moricière. La Moricière and his senior officers attempted to rein in the panic but to no avail. However, a battalion of Austrian Bersaglieri from Pimodan's reserve remained steadfast as they maneuvered toward the Upper Farm. But, it was not enough to push back the Piedmontese. La Moricière ordered a retreat back to the Lower Farm.

The Lower Farm quickly developed into hand-to-hand combat. For a moment, despite other units fleeing, the Franco-Belgians and the newly arrived Austrian Bersaglieri were able to stop the advance of the Piedmontese. However, this small victory was short lived and it became clear that it was only a matter of time before the Piedmontese would force the Pontificals back to Loreto.

Trying to salvage as much of his original plan as possible, La Moricière left to find elements of his scattered troops to rally them on the road to Ancona. Colonel Goudenhoven was left in charge, and he quickly realized there was little they could do, so he ordered a retreat back to Loreto.

In the confusion of the retreat two dozen Franco-Belgian soldiers alongside several wounded soldiers, including Pimodan, were left in the Lower Farm. They fought off three assaults on their position and held out for more than an hour after all other Pontifical units had left. They finally surrendered the house around 2:00 pm.

When the remainder of Pimodan's forces reached Loreto defensive positions were quickly set up. Of the 6,800 men who departed earlier that morning only 2,000 returned, most of the rest were captured. There were so many casualties that the Sanctuary of the Holy House of Loreto was turned into a temporary hospital.

That evening Colonel Goudenhoven convened a council of war with his remaining officers. The French, Belgian, Austrian, and Irish officers wanted to fight to the last man at Loreto. However, the Swiss and Italians, which consisted of at least half of the remaining force, lost the will to fight. Therefore, in the morning, the Papal forces surrendered Loreto with the agreement that they be given the honors of war and officers allowed to retain their swords.

La Moricière meanwhile, had managed to gather around 450 men, and they quickly made their way to Ancona. However, along the way they were discovered by the Italians. Most of the small Papal force held off the attack while La Moricière, a few of his aides, and cavalry troopers escaped to Ancona. Upon entering the city La Moricière said "I no long have an army."

The battle was over, and the loss was so catastrophic that it came to be known as a massacre and the fallen Papal Soldiers as martyrs. The field was filled with so many noble Catholic youth of France that an Italian General commented, "You would think this was a list of invites for a ball given by Louis XIV!"

The Papal Army lost 88 men, including Pimodan, and had more than 400 wounded. Out of the 270 that fought in the Franco-Belgian Battalion, only 91 returned unscathed. Around 120 were wounded, 30 were taken prisoner, and 30 were killed. The Piedmontese lost 62 men and had 140 wounded. There are many reasons for the Papal loss. For example, their weapons were less advanced, as they had mostly smooth bore rifles and artillery compared with the new rifle barreling the Piedmontese had.

Additionally, at the start, the Papal forces overestimated the amount of Piedmontese they were engaged with, believing they were outnumbered. When in actuality the Pontificals had 6,800 fighting men directly on the battlefield compared to 4,800 Piedmontese. The Papal forces failed to capitalize on their numerical advantage by splitting into three columns. This led to only a small numerical advantage in most of their engagements. For example, when they reached the crest of Musone hill the first time it was 1,600 Pontificals versus 1,200 Piedmontese. Additionally, this likely negatively affected their morale, especially for the native units.

However, when the Piedmontese reserve regiment arrived the Papal Army lost their numerical advantage for the remainder of the battle, this was part of the reason they were driven from the crest of the hill back to the Upper Farm. When accounting for the artillery, support, and reserve elements of Caldini's IV Corps there were actually around 16,500 Piedmontese engaged in the battle.

Considering the armies as a whole, the Pontificals were vastly outnumbered, with a fighting force of around 13,000 compared to Piedmont's 70,000 soldiers. Meaning that even if the Papal Army was successful at Castelfidardo. They would have still been significantly outnumbered at Ancona.

The terrain was another factor. The Piedmontese had the advantage since the Papal force had to fight uphill. Tired from battling uphill for hours and losing their numerical advantage it is no surprise that the Piedmontese were able to repel the Papal advance and send them back downhill. This also had detrimental effects on the Papal artillery as it had to be dragged up and down continuously, thereby reducing its effectiveness. Upon their retreat, the river proved to be another frustrating factor, as it slowed down the Papal retreat causing further confusion and loss of life.

Another reason and perhaps the most important was that the Papal Army was far less experienced and trained, especially when compared to the Army of Sardinia-Piedmont, which was one of the most well trained in Europe at the time and also utilized conscription to bolster its numbers. Up to this point, the Papal Army for centuries lacked training, resources, and manpower. When considering that the Minister of War Monsignor Xavier de Mérode and Papal Army Commander General de la Moricière had spent less than a year reforming the Papal Army, things could have been much worse.

Finally, there was the tactical error from La Moricière in choosing to deviate from the original mission, which was a fix and bypass. By committing his column to the battle instead of bypassing to Ancona, the mission essentially became an attack to seize. His column did little to change the outcome of the battle, and instead resulted in a significantly reduced reinforcement force that arrived in Ancona. Though, in the grand scheme of things, it probably wouldn't have made much of a difference since no Catholic powers came to the aid of the Papal States at Ancona. The Papal Army held out at Ancona until the 29th. With the last of the Papal forces surrendered, the Crusade of 1860 ended and with it, the reduction of the Papal States to the Lazio region.

Despite the loss and mistakes of the Papal Army, the martyrdom and glorious sacrifice of the Papal Soldiers isn't lessened.

Indeed, as you will read in this book, the soldiers offered themselves to the service of the Pope despite overwhelming odds. They were ready to suffer and die as witnesses to Christ and His Church, against an army motivated by hatred for the Pope and his temporal power, all for the sake of uniting Italy under the flag of Piedmont.

Indeed, their fellow soldiers considered their fallen comrades as martyrs. Their stories served as an inspiration for the Papal Army over the course of the next decade as they continued to defend the Papal States until the fall of Rome on September 20, 1870. One of the soldiers even had a packet prepared by his diocese to champion his cause for Sainthood. The story of Joseph-Louis Guerin's martyrdom will be discussed in a chapter toward the end of the book. After his death, over 30 miraculous healings were attributed to his intercession. Bl. Pope Pius IX even placed a portrait of Guerin in the antechamber of his private chapel in Castel-Gandolfo and it was under his invitation that the Bishop of Nantes began putting a packet together for Guerin in 1862.

Unfortunately, beyond a packet his cause was not pursued, he became a victim of the political climate of the time. Due to the precarious situation with the Papal States, some felt it was not appropriate to potentially anger Napolean III by canonizing a Papal soldier that embodied the values of royalism and monarchism. During this time the Papal States relied on a garrison of French soldiers in Rome to dissuade the Piedmontese from trying another invasion. In 1925 his cause was reconsidered but the political climate prevented the process from moving forward again, this time due to the condemnation of Action Française by Pope Pius XI in 1926. It is one of the hopes of the author, that this book will help re-establish the cult of Joseph-Louis Guerin and breathe new life into his cause.

The Martyrs of Castelfidardo was written by Marquis de Ségur in 1861, about a year after the Battle of Castelfidardo. The book became an inspiration for many Frenchmen to join the Papal Zouaves. An English translation by a member of the Presentation convent in Kerry, Ireland was made in 1883. An illustrated French version of the book was re-published in 1891 with engravings by Felix Bouisset. The editor has combined, for the first time, the illustrations from the 1891 version with the English translation in 1883. The English translation has also been changed to reflect American grammar. For example, words like "colour" have been changed to "color." Please enjoy reading the exploits, heroism, and sacrifice of *The Martyrs of Castelfidardo*. Re-released for the first time in over 100 years!

Bl. Pius IX. Pope-King.

DEDICATION

TO THE MOTHERS, WIVES, AND SISTERS OF those Christian heroes who have given their lives for the Holy See, on the field of Castelfidardo, I dedicate this book. They have participated in their sacrifice by their self-denial, devotedness, and heroic courage; and, whilst their sons, their husbands, and their brothers have consummated their glorious martyrdom, they silently continue theirs in loneliness and tears.

Having had so large a part in their pain, they will one day enjoy the recompense which these soldiers of Jesus Christ already enjoy in heaven; they have likewise a right to share with them the admiration and gratitude of the Catholic world. Writers of fiction immortalize the heroes of their works, no matter how vulgar they may be. As for me, what I wish and hope is that the imperishable glory of those martyrs, whose acts I am going to relate, may communicate to my words something of its luster and duration. May these pages, written from my heart, serve to console those widowed souls to whom I dedicate them. May these noble and holy women accept the respectful and grateful homage of a Frenchman, and a Catholic, who, like them, is indignant at the outrages heaped upon our august Pontiff, and the misfortunes of Holy Church; who has wept with them over so many noble young men, cut down in the flower of their youth on the plains of Castelfidardo; but who, like them, hopes against hope; and, recalling the eternal promises made to Peter and his successors, remembers that Calvary preceded the Resurrection; and knowing how potent the blood of martyrs is, when weighed in the balance of divine mercy, awaits with calm and unshaken confidence the perhaps not far distant day, which will witness the complete triumph of the Holy, Catholic, Apostolic, and Roman Church.

A. DE SEGUR
19th January, 1881

PREFACE

THIS BOOK IS NOT A HISTORY OF THE Italian Revolution, nor of the Roman question. It is not even the history of the Pontifical Army. It is simply the story of the acts of the French martyrs of Castelfidardo, that is to say, of those young heroes, those noble volunteers, who left France to defend the Holy See, and who either fell on the battlefield, or died afterwards from the effects of their wounds. I would wish that this outline contained the names of all those who gave their lives in this holy cause, no matter to what nation they belonged, but the documents were too defective to realize such a project in a satisfactory manner; therefore, as the glory of France and the memory of her children interest me in a special manner, I have limited myself to collecting and writing that which concerns our glorious compatriots, and to recognizing the dead, the illustrious and well-beloved dead, of France on the battlefield of Castelfidardo, like to those Christians of the first ages, who, gliding in the dusk of evening into the amphitheater after the combats of the day, gathered, on bended knees, and weeping, the relics of their martyrs.

THE
MARTYRS
OF
CASTELFIDARDO

CHAPTER I
MARTYRS

N THIS AGE OF CONFUSION AND TROUBLE the glorious name of martyr is everywhere perverted and misapplied. It is profaned by the revolutionists, who apply it to the most miserable wretches, from Marat and Robespierre, martyrs of popular passion, to the assassins of emperors and kings, martyrs of the Italian idea. But we must not be astonished; Satan (this ape of God, as a great writer designates him), who, although he cannot create, imitates and wishes to have his martyrs, just as God has His apostles and saints. Besides impious men who profane the most sacred names, there are certain well-meaning men who dishonor this name by using it without discretion. The most vulgar devotion suffices in order to be declared holy by an infuriated mob, yet they deny the name to those who have suffered persecution and contradiction even in a just cause. It is not in this degraded sense that I comprehend this great name which I have written on the first page of this work. In the Catholic sense of the word, a martyr is a Christian, who, having given testimony to the truth by shedding his blood, enters through his sacrifice into the glory of eternal happiness.

Now, such have been, according to all appearances, the heroes of this brief but immortal day of Castelfidardo. They have given their blood for the cause of the Pope, they have given it joyfully, willingly: not alone with the resignation of faith, but with the eagerness of sacrifice. To die for the Pope is to die for the Church, to die for the Church is to die for God, and to die for God is to be born to eternal life. They have, then, undoubtedly been martyrs, and have passed from the field of battle or their bloody couch in the hospital to the joys of paradise. This is what our Holy Father Pius IX and all the bishops of the Catholic world have given expression to in their panegyrics over the graves of those heroic young men. Likewise, under similar circumstances, eight centuries ago, Pope Leo IX, of glorious

3

memory, one of the most illustrious predecessors of Pius IX. also witnessed young men die for the Church. Here let me recall this beautiful and touching, though too often forgotten page of Church history, which bears so divine a resemblance to that which has been written in our own time in letters of blood and glory on the plains of Castelfidardo:

> In the year 1053, the Normans, greedy of plunder, took away from the Holy See the Duchy of Benevento; they brought ruin and devastation on convents, churches, and even on those holy shrines which had formerly been the objects of their pilgrimages. The Sovereign Pontiff, wishing to stop their depredations, and persuaded that his condition of king obliged him to have recourse to arms, summoned the Italians to rally round him. In the following terms he makes known his determination to the Emperor of Constantinople: 'Since nothing has been able to stop the excesses of these people, neither censures, nor exhortations, nor prayers, I have resolved to employ human means, and to expose myself in order to deliver from these outrages the flock committed to me by Jesus Christ.' Firm in his resolution the holy Pontiff marched against the enemy with a small army composed of German cavalry, Lombard lancers, and foot soldiers from various parts of Italy. They repaired to the province of Capitanate, where the Normans concentrated their forces; but failing in provisions, and fearing the disastrous issue of a combat, they sued for peace. They sent deputies to the Pope promising to pay an annual tribute, and refrain from all hostilities, if he would give them possession of the country which they had already taken away from the Church.
>
> The Pope, as a contemporary author attests, answered them by a dignified and noble refusal. The Normans immediately prepared to give battle. The engagement took place on the 18th of June, 1053, near Dragonara. The onset was terrible: the pontifical army was defeated; the Germans would not yield, but died sword in hand to the last man. Covered with blood and dust, maddened by such a dearly bought victory, the Normans hastened to Civitella, where the Sovereign

4

Pontiff had taken refuge. They set fire to the cottages outside the town, and thus forced the Vicar of Jesus Christ to leave his retreat. Preceded by the cross he went straight up to his enemies. At the sight of the holy Pontiff, who had always treated them with benignity, and to whose virtues misfortune added new luster, these fierce warriors threw themselves on the ground weeping. Several of them dragged themselves along on their knees to his feet in order to receive his benediction and hear his words. Without any resentment for the afflictions which they had caused him, and with the simplicity of a dove, the Pope, stopping in the midst of them, recommended them to bring forth worthy fruits of penance; and after having received from them an oath that they would be his faithful vassals instead of those knights they had killed, gave them his benediction.

The Pope then repaired to the battlefield, where were lying a great number of his relatives and friends. On seeing their mutilated remains he was deeply affected, calling them by their names, and wishing that he had died with them. One thing, however, struck him, the bodies of his soldiers were intact, whilst those of the Normans were already half-devoured by wild beasts. The Pontiff regarded this remarkable occurrence as an assurance of the eternal salvation of those who died for him, and afforded him no small consolation in his bitter grief. He spent two days on the battlefield in fasting and prayer, and made the Normans inter the bodies in a neighboring church, where he celebrated the office for the dead. Returning to Benevento a prey to sadness, which the remembrance of those noble souls, who died fighting for him, caused, he daily offered the adorable sacrifice for the repose of their souls; but one day he had a vision in which he was ordered to pray no longer for them, and hence forth to consider them as martyrs. Wibert de Toul, contemporary biographer of Leo IX, adds, that it was revealed several times to this holy Pontiff that those generous defenders of the Church were enjoying the happiness of heaven; because they voluntarily submitted to death for the faith of Jesus Christ, and the deliverance of an oppressed Christian people. They themselves appeared at intervals to several of the faithful, and told them no longer to weep or surround their remains with funeral attire, as they now enjoyed eternal glory.

These revelations were afterwards confirmed, not alone by different miracles wrought through their intercession, but by a vision which the holy Pontiff had in his last illness. Worn out by a long and tedious malady, and feeling the approach of death, he called around him some bishops and priests and spoke to them thus: The hour of my death is fast approaching, for I have had this night a vision in which I saw the heavenly Jerusalem, and as I looked with astonishment at the scene before me, I saw all those who had died for the Church of Jesus Christ numbered among the martyrs; their clothes were resplendent like gold; they held in their hands palms bearing everlasting flowers, and all called aloud to me, saying: Come and dwell with us, for it is through you we have acquired this glory. 'Then a voice from the other side replied: Not yet, but in three days thou wilt be reunited to us; here is thy place, thy throne is prepared and awaits thee.' Three days after, according to the revelation, the holy Pontiff gave up his soul in peace to God."

Thus it was that, eight hundred years ago, the Sovereign Judge and dispenser of all things, He who rewards the good and punishes the wicked, revealed to his representative here below, and through him to the entire Catholic world, that those who die in defense of the rights of the Holy See are really and truly martyrs.

Then, as the Church cannot err, the victims of 1860 have a right to this glorious title as well as those of 1053; their cause was the same: it was the cause of God and the Pope. The malice of the assailants is greater, what do I say? it is a hundred times greater; but so also is the Catholic devotion of these defenders of the Holy See. On one side it is always a race of plunderers, hypocrites, ambitious men, enemies of all justice, blood-thirsty followers of Satan, who was a liar and a murderer from the beginning; on the other, it is always the race of the valiant and noble, those who die in the simplicity of their faith and devotion, the race of the Maccabees and Crusaders, ever living in the Church of Jesus Christ.[*]

As for the rest it is an old struggle, which was born with the world, and will only end with it. The Spouse of Jesus Christ has always to combat for her Divine Spouse against the powers of darkness. These powers have had different names according to their time and place. At Jerusalem they were known by the names of Judas, Caiphas, Herod, and Pilate. At Rome they were known by the names of Nero, Decius, Diocletian, and Julian the Apostate. Later on they have taken the names of Arius, Mahomet, etc. In our own day they are known by an all-encompassing name, specifically *Revolution!* But no matter under what name, it is always the same struggle, the struggle of evil against good; of the flesh against the spirit; of barbarism, more or less refined, against Christian civilization.

Italy is the battlefield where these two great armies meet. At the head of each are chiefs worthy of their posts. On one side our most holy and venerated Father and Pontiff, Pope Pius IX, a lion in energy, a lamb in meekness, dignified and majestic even in his misfortunes. On the other side there is the king Victor Emmanuel, sacrilegious offspring of a pious race, who bears in his brazen features a striking resemblance to Henry VIII, who plundered and dethroned the King of Naples whilst calling him his cousin, and the Sovereign Pontiff whilst calling him his Father. And Garibaldi, the revolutionist, that is to say the demolisher by essence, the breaker of doors which were opened by cowardice or treason, who engages himself for gold, followed by his excommunicated band, and escorted by his worthy almoner, the apostate priest Gavazzi; Garibaldi, the sworn enemy of the Church and France; less repugnant, however, than the gallant king and his genteel ministers, because he is neither a king nor a gentleman, because he is ignorant and rash, because he says haughtily what he thinks and wishes, and instead of hiding his revolutionary projects under a golden robe or a black coat, he audaciously wears a red shirt, worthy emblem of his aspirations. This terrible child of Revolution has

---

[*] The brilliant miracles which take place daily at the tomb of the Pontifical Zouave, Joseph Guerin, proves that God deems the martyrs of Castelfidardo worthy successors of the martyrs of Dragonara. (*Author's note*)

told us its aim and object, which will remain forever as the program and brand of this war of Italian unity:

> The Papacy is the canker worm of Italy; it must be extirpated. The most redoubtable enemy of our country is the Priest; we must stone him!*

Such were their savage and impious cries; such was the aim of the Revolution, and it is against this sacrilegious design, these impious and sanguinary words that the volunteers of Castelfidardo have fought. It was the Papacy, it was the Priest whose seat was at Rome they rushed to defend, knowing well that the members are dishonored and fettered when the head is a captive and outraged.

Behold why the Church has already saluted them with the title of martyrs; and an illustrious bishop has said without the least exaggeration, "that the blood which they shed was the purest of France." In saying that it was the purest he did not mean that it was the noblest. Bishops are accustomed to recall to the minds of the great and the little, the sovereign and the subject, that they will be all weighed in the same balance, and judged by the same God; therefore, they make no such distinction in their sentiments of grief and admiration. But their blood was the purest, because it was so truly Catholic, that is to say, most devoted, and flowed from chaste and faithful hearts, who voluntarily offered to shed it in a thrice holy cause, the cause of the Sovereign Pontiff, of Christian civilization, and the honor of France!

And now that the enemies of the Holy See calumniate them by the name of mercenaries, and thus judging them by their own standard transform into party spirit their pure and unalloyed devotion to their religion, we shall merely answer them in the following words: "Read the acts of these martyrs, their farewell letters to their mothers, the accounts of their last moments, and if you have still a spark of faith left you, you will strike your breast and exclaim with us, or rather with the entire episcopacy: 'No, these heroic young men have not fallen victims to their political passions, they are the martyrs of the Catholic Faith, the immortal martyrs of the Papacy!'"

---

* Garibaldi ended by raising the mask, and mingles the name of France and the Emperor with his furious imprecations against the Papacy.

CHAPTER II

THE PONTIFICAL ARMY—LORETTO—CASTELFIDARDO

HE OBJECT OF THIS WORK BEING exclusively religious, my aim, therefore is not to relate the history of the Italian war, its origin, its catastrophes, its present or future results. I think it necessary, however, to recall briefly the circumstances which preceded, accompanied, and followed the formation of the pontifical army, and which ended in the battle of Castelfidardo and the taking of Ancona. Nothing will more vividly show the purely Catholic character of this campaign, which we justly term the crusade of 1860. Surrounded by enemies whose object was the destruction of his temporal and spiritual power, the Pope could not yield his rights, nor those of the Catholic world without a struggle; neither could he resist alone those revolutionists come from the four points of the compass. To do so two things were necessary, which Italy did not produce, namely, generals and soldiers. Knowing that in defending his temporal sovereignty he defended the rampart of his spiritual authority, and the supreme asylum of Catholic liberty, he considered it was the duty of Catholics to protect their common patrimony, and without challenging them accepted their devotedness. As France had always borne the beautiful title of "Eldest Daughter of the Church," as she had in ages past the principal part in the recognition and support of the temporal power of the Roman Pontiff; as, on the other hand, she had been always fruitful in valiant soldiers and intrepid generals, our Holy Father Pius IX thought proper to ask from this Catholic and devoted land the chief of the army which he was calling to defend him. This chief was General de la Moricière, and the choice troop which followed him soon came to be known as the Franco-Belgian Battalion. A fervent Catholic, General de la Moricière wished in accepting the mandate of the Holy Father to make it purely a religious act; as, had he weighed the matter from a human point of view, he would most certainly have

General de la Moricière.

refused it. Success was too doubtful, and the dishonorable character of his enemies too apparent. "The Pope asks me, I must obey," was his answer to the envoy of the Sovereign Pontiff, and the next day he left his noble wife, who was worthy of encouraging his devotion, and his cherished children, and set out for Rome. Conqueror of Abd-el-Kader in Africa, of Socialism in Paris, he brought to the cause of the Holy See a mind capable of appreciating the dignity of his mission, a consummate military experience, a courage proverbial even in the French army, and the support of a popular name, that injuries, puns, and calumnies could not tarnish.

Following his example, an army of volunteers offered themselves to the Sovereign Pontiff, and the Franco-Belgian Battalion (the only one of which I shall speak here) was quickly formed. Instead of a few hundred soldiers France would have given thousands, if, on the one hand, the days of chivalry had not passed, and, on the other, if the Holy Father through noble and paternal sentiments had not kept silence, which left a doubt as to his real intentions. Whatever it may have been, there were enough of French volunteers at Castelfidardo to stop for a moment the entire Piedmontese army, and add a beautiful page to the history of France, and a holy page to the history of the Church.

That which I wish to establish without doubt is, that all these noble young men left their families, their country, their wealth, through pure and unalloyed devotion to the cause of the Church. From the glorious and immortal General de Pimodan to the poor Breton peasant, all had but one thought, one desire to fight, to suffer, even to die, for the Pope and Holy Church. This fixed idea, if I may thus express it, was to be found in their letters, their conversations, in their parting words when setting out for Rome, and even in their last moments when rendering their pure souls to God. It was the thought of mothers when embracing their sons, of wives in separating from their husbands, of sisters when saying the last fond adieu (Goodbye forever) to their brothers.

"I have no money to give our Holy Father," said a noble child of Nantes; "but instead of money I can give my life, and I offer it to him with all my heart."

Meeting of Pius IX and La Moricière.

"I confess to you," writes another, "that it is not a decoration from Pius IX that I ambition; I have more elevated views: it is the martyr's palm I am seeking. In a word, whatever be the fate God has in store for me, pray for me, and keep up your heart. I am obeying an inspiration from on high." Such were the sentiments of those volunteers. See now what were those of the mothers of those young heroes:

"Go, my child," said one of them to her only son, when asking her permission to join the volunteers, "and may God bless you. For more than a month I have prayed Him to send you this inspiration." And another, answering the objections of a friend, who showed her in perspective the death of her son, replied:

"It is not necessary that my son should live, but it is necessary to defend the Holy See." Such were the sentiments which pervaded this crusade, and the consequences have been worthy of such a beginning.

We can imagine what those noble volunteers had to suffer during their three months' sojourn in Italy, the greater number of whom were brought up in luxury. I shall not speak of the hard life which they had to spend during their multiplied exercises; their forced marches across the Roman States, in order to supply by the rapidity of movements the insufficiency of numbers. I shall not speak of the inadequateness of their temporary barracks, the want of the plainest food, which even the countryman leaving his farm to join the garrison has; all these trials, though hard to bear, were as nothing to our brave French men. But they had also to bear other trials, namely, the vexation of being misunderstood, insulted, calumniated, by those who call themselves Frenchmen; the irksomeness of hearing themselves railed at and cursed by several of those very Romans whom they came to protect. There were cowards who understood not their courage; egotists who did not comprehend their devotion, and this vile race is perhaps more numerous in Italy than elsewhere. Well, these brave young men supported all this heroically, joyfully, never allowing their courage or cheerfulness to flag or their faith to falter. One of them, escaping from the massacre of Castelfidardo, and being questioned on this point on his return to France, replied with noble simplicity:

"Oh! we paid no attention to these things: we were Christians." Another, escaping likewise from the combat, but a prisoner in the hands of the Piedmontese, wrote thus:

"We have offered ourselves; God has not willed to accept all; however, in waiting, we can continue our sacrifice, and if they spit in our faces we will think of our Divine Master."

Christians when departing, Christians in the regiment, they were also Christians in the combat. I will not here repeat what everyone knows the deceitful promises of the Piedmontese, followed by unheard of crimes, the violation of oaths, the immediate and sacrilegious invasion of the Papal States by their armies, which were reunited on the frontiers under the pretext of preventing their invasion by the Garibaldians, and this infamous attack embellished by the name of "The Campaign of the Marches and Umbria," ending in the assassination of the little army of the Pope. Neither shall I recall how de la Moricière, surrounded all at once, and on all sides, by clouds of enemies, rejecting as dishonorable the thought of surrendering without combat, resolved to make one desperate effort to make a way through the enemies' lines to Ancona. But I wish to show how these Christian soldiers prepared to combat and die for the Church; and in order to do so perfectly, I will allow a holy priest, who was at Loretto on the eve of the battle, relate those admirable deeds which Providence permitted he should witness:

"I started from Rome for Loretto on Wednesday the 12th September, accompanied by M. l'Abbé.* We did not think the war would break out before being declared and accepted, and besides we did not wish to delay the accomplishment of our pilgrimage. However, on Friday morning, the 14th instant, as we were ascending the hill of Assisi, we heard loud detonations of artillery. Some country people said to us: "These are the Piedmontese quarreling with General Schmidt. You may guess our thoughts. The Church of Jesus Christ was being attacked with a dishonesty and cowardice which recalled to us the last scenes of the Passion. The Piedmontese were the Jews. We addressed ourselves with tears to St. Francis, the admirable

---

* M. stands for Monsieur and is the French way of saying Mr. MM. stands for Messieurs and is the plural form of M. Mme. Stands for Madame, and is the French way of saying Mrs.

and faithful copy of the sufferings of our Lord, beseeching him by his holy wounds to have pity on our friends and enemies. I cannot describe to you my feelings when I heard the booming of the cannon whilst celebrating the sacred mysteries on the tomb of the patriarch of Assisi. About mid-day we descended to Santa Maria degli Angeli, where our carriage was waiting, and in a short time we arrived at Foligno: it was a market day, the streets were crowded. Confiding in the Holy Virgin, and certain of help from France, we continued our way towards Loretto.

"At eleven o'clock at night, near Tolentino, we found Pimodan's troops bivouacked. The soldiers were resting in their tents, full of ardent courage. The next day, Saturday, we reached Tolentino early. The churches were crowded, the priests busily engaged hearing confessions, and distributing Holy Communion. Many soldiers were mingled amongst the faithful. It was consoling to think that so many souls were united in the love of Jesus Christ and His Church. At noon we met at Macerata the noble General de la Moricière with the bulk of his army. In a moment we were surrounded by the guides (The Guides of la Moricière were a unit of Cavalry Scouts) and by the Franco-Belgians, who one and all manifested the most heroic sentiments. They had but one feeling, love for the Church; one aim, the triumph of the Church. Towards evening we reached Loretto, where we were told that Cialdini, with a large army, occupied Asimo and Jesi. In fact, you could see the numerous fires of this army glittering, and fugitives related that they had counted more than twenty thousand men, which would be trebled in two days. We were expecting the arrival of de la Moricière and Pimodan, when about two o'clock a detachment of eighty Piedmontese lancers entered the town accompanied by some miscreants disguised and odious to behold. Their object was to excite the people. A great commotion prevailed. A tall man, with disheveled hair and beard, held under his arm a bundle of tricolor banners, which he distributed to the shopkeepers of the Grande Rue, with an air which was quickly understood; then he drew from the deep pockets of his coat Piedmontese cockades.

I never saw a transformation so rapid; the town was in one instant decked with flags, and cowards donned the cockade

A tall man, with dishevelled hair and beard...

in the twinkling of an eye. I heard people who had spoken to me in the morning of their love for the Pope cry with all their might, "Long live Victor Emmanuel!" Our innkeeper, whose good feelings appeared to us to be carried away by the exaltation of the moment, laid aside his black coat for a lighter costume. Decked out in a sort of helmet adorned with a cockade he commenced unfastening the arms of the Sovereign Pontiff, which were placed over the door of his inn, called "The Bell," which, by the way, was a posting establishment also. But in five hours the scene was changed: "La Moricière! behold La Moricière! Long live La Moricière!" re-echoed on every side. And there was the Christian general; his troops walking with a martial tread, because they believed Loretto to be in the power of the enemy. The guides were leading, and the ardent desire to combat for Holy Church sparkled in every eye. The banners and cockades disappeared, if possible, more quickly than they had appeared, and cries of "Viva Pio Nono! Viva il generale! Viva la Moricière!" resounded through the air. All this awakened in me many sad reflections regarding the fickleness of these poor Italian people.

Such is the way with those who sometimes by base flattery, unparalleled infamy, or parricidal aggressions pretend to give assurances of liberty and independence. Where can honor or faith be found there? Soon our innkeeper reappeared in the gravest apparel; with tears in his eyes. He spoke to us of his devotion to the holy cause, and assured us that he had been constrained to act as he did a few hours before, beseeching us, at the same time, to obtain for him from Moricière a generous pardon. In a few minutes the little army was encamped on the square and in the streets. Five guides were sent to reconnoiter on the Asimo road, in order to ascertain if the bridge was cut or not; amongst these was the young Mizaël de Pas of Arras. His arm being broken by a bullet, he was brought to the Jesuits' college. We were present at the first dressing of his wound, which he suffered with angelic resignation, murmuring words of gratitude to God for having deigned to choose him as one of the first victims immolated to His cause. Ah! how noble did this young Christian appear to me, and how detestable the Piedmontese! M. de Pas edified his

17

companions-in-arms by his piety and virtue. He did not survive his wound, but after a few days of intense sufferings, died at Loretto. If his mother, of whom he spoke with the greatest veneration, should chance to see these lines, let her know, that whilst compassionating her we envy her, as she has given to the Church one of the worthiest of heroes and the most amiable of victims. On Monday we expected Pimodan's column, which soon arrived at the port of Ricanati. It seemed to me that the Piedmontese could easily defeat them; but Providence willed that the trial should be made at the time, and in the place He had chosen for the greater glory of His defenders, and the manifestation of His justice.

"I had the honor of offering the Holy Sacrifice on the altar of the Holy House. The basilica was full of officers and soldiers, who knelt, without distinction of rank, at the holy table. I spent the day amongst them, feeling myself penetrated with respect and admiration at the sight of so much valor and faith. "Monsieur l'Abbé," said the French, "we are delighted the hour of combat approaches. The plains and hills around Loretto are covered with Piedmontese, and to this army of sixty-thousand men we are but a handful. Perhaps we shall be killed, but they shall not triumph; our blood and our lives will not be uselessly given, and God will reward our families and our country." In the evening Generals Moricière and Pimodan, and nearly all the officers and soldiers, prepared to encounter the peril of battle by approaching the tribunal of penance. Several having asked me to hear their confessions, I obtained permission from the Bishop of Loretto, and I bless God for having thus enabled me, at this supreme moment, to assist so many noble and holy children of France. At daybreak on Tuesday there was a scene worthy of the epoch of the Crusades, and which, as a priest and a Frenchman, gave me the greatest consolation. At four o'clock Moricière, Pimodan, and all the staff-officers, the guides, and the German regiments, the foreigners and natives, all received Holy Communion. I saw the greater number of them prostrate in prayer; amongst others I remarked M. de Bourbon Charlus, who remained a long time in this suppliant posture. In the recollection of the two generals there was something so grave and solemn, that I could not master my emotion; besides I saw around me faces bathed in tears. On leaving the church, one of the Swiss said to me:

"Here is a letter for mother. Pray for us, Monsieur l'Abbe; we are going to shed our blood for the Pope and Church." I heard afterwards that the noble young man was killed; and I then sent his letter, with a few lines from myself, to his poor mother. Several of my compatriots gave me their letters to forward to their friends. On the ramparts, towards the north side of the plain, perceiving a movement amongst the enemy's troops, which seemed like a swarm of ants in the distance, the Franco-Belgians said to me: "Bless us, Monsieur l'Abbe, for we shall never meet again on earth." And they spoke truly.

Half an hour before their departure, the General called on my traveling companion and myself, and said to us: "You will return to Rome; tell M. de Merode to send us some provisions to Ancona; we hope to be there this evening. Our numbers are a unit in comparison to our enemies; but we trust in the Holy Virgin." They brought with them from the Holy House the banners of Lepanto. We wished to see this little body of troops file off, a holy and sublime image of the Church Militant. Glory and honor shone in their faces, and we remained standing with our heads uncovered. "We ought to kneel down," said my companion to me, "they are martyrs." We exchanged looks, and pressed each other's hands. As our *vetturino* (coach) awaited us, we left Loretto, begging of God, and His Holy Mother, to assist their defenders. When we were about three kilometers from the town we heard the firing commence, then the cannon. Ah, how these shots pierced our hearts! The booming of the cannon plaintively re-echoed in the hearts of all Catholics and well-meaning people, for it denoted the massacre of the Pontifical Army; the defeat of the holiest rights; the triumph of brutal force, treachery, and sacrilege, on the ruins of justice, true Christian civilization, and European honor. The Pope's army was not conquered, but assassinated; and the evening of that day which has left a bloody page in the history of the world, found General de la Moricière, followed by a hundred men who had pierced through with him the Piedmontese army, entering Ancona; they were all that remained of the army of Castelfidardo; the rest were either killed, wounded,

View of Ancona.

or prisoners. The troops of General Pimodan, composed of Germans, Swiss, and Franco-Belgian carabineers, supported, almost alone, the weight of this eventful day. These valiant soldiers fought like lions, and made the Piedmontese pay dearly for their shame-bought victory. Everywhere in advance the Franco-Belgians performed prodigies of valor and daring, and we may apply to them the words of the poet:

> The combat only ceased,
> For want of combatants.

We shall let one of the heroes of this sacred battalion speak:[*]

"Our battalion, springing forward with the greatest intrepidity, crossed, under a shower of balls, a deep ravine, and in a few moments were ranged in order of battle on the opposite side. Just then our brave commander's horse was killed by a bullet. According to the orders of our chief, we drove back the skirmishers, who, dislodged from their position, did us great harm by repeated firing. At the point of the bayonet we carried a position occupied by the enemy, and which became the tomb of the greater number of our brothers-in-arms. Our commander, judging this situation a very important point, gave orders to have us establish ourselves there. We took possession of an abandoned farm-house, and then commenced the frightful drama, which ended in our captivity. Several strong columns of the enemy's troops succeeded in repulsing a few of our brave men who were rushing forward, but stopped by our firing, which proceeded from every window in the house, they could not pursue them far, and, therefore, were compelled to retreat with enormous loss.

"The struggle then concentrated around us; a new column, composed entirely of *bersaglieri*, was repulsed, and the earth strewed with their dead bodies. In fine, the enemy seeing they could not dislodge us without considerable loss, laid regular siege to our position. This was real carnage: bullets, bombs, and grape-shot soon disabled numbers of our men, and four of our officers were mortally wounded. A few of our enemies

---

[*] Corporal Arthur Guillemin, he later promoted to Lieutenant and was killed in the campaign of 1867 at the Battle of Monte-Libretti

Arthur Guillemin.

were wounded, amongst whom was one officer. We could have prolonged the struggle some minutes but for the falling of an incendiary bomb, and as the house contained inflammable matter, it was soon in a blaze. There was now no choice left us but to surrender, or be buried in ruins. Willingly would we have died, but our dying officers and brothers-in-arms were imploring aid, and besides, our chiefs decided on our surrendering. We had done our duty; the white flag was hoisted, and, in a few minutes after, those who survived this dreadful butchery, were defiled in the midst of the enemy's ranks. Several of these intrepid combatants were quite young, almost children, and their lion-like courage was occasionally mingled with sentiments of amiability and good nature. Whilst besieged in the farm-house, which was transformed by their courage into a fortress, holding in check an entire army of assailants, looking from behind the Venetian blinds, where they could see without being seen, these heroic young men used to say to one another; 'Ah! how can I shoot this poor child? Perhaps he has a mother who will weep for him. What do you say? I do not know what to do.' Again: 'Oh! look at him; he is so young! What a misfortune to kill him.' 'Listen, my dear fellow, if you do not kill him, he will, perhaps, kill you, and you have a mother!'"

It was thus everywhere, even on the battlefield, that these Christian soldiers showed they were imbued with noble and humane feelings. It was on their bed of pain, where many of them finished their martyrdom, that their noble characters were shown in bold relief. It is there, when the heat of the battle is over, when the excitement has ceased, when the dream of glory gives place to that of slow and painful suffering, that the man appears such as he really is, and shows his true character. It is there the true greatness of the Christian soul is proved, in that patience which endures all, in that faith which rejoices in everything, in that love of God which actuates all. I dare to assert that not one of those noble heroes of Castelfidardo were found wanting in this hour of supreme trial. The hospital found them greater still than the battlefield, but all embraced their sufferings with that holy joy of the predestined. They reposed on their bed of pain as on a nuptial couch, singing canticles of eternal love. It was thus in the primitive ages of the Church that the confessors of the Faith awaited in their dungeons the consummation of their sacrifice, full of joy, hope, and humility. Here I cannot resist transcribing a page written by an eye-witness, about seventeen hundred years ago, so closely does it resemble the history of our dear wounded ones of Castelfidardo:

"In the year 174, the Christians of Lyons, worn out by punishments, awaited death in those dark dungeons, where they were heaped together. All covered with wounds, which they had received through love of Jesus Christ, they could not bear to be called martyrs, and whenever they were styled thus by persons conversing with them, they were greatly afflicted, and reprimanded them sweetly but strongly. 'This glorious name,' they said, 'belongs only to those who have finished their course, and whom Jesus Christ has taken to Himself in the midst of their torments, and not to vile creatures like us.' Then, taking our hands and watering them with their tears, they implored of us to obtain for them by our prayers the grace of final perseverance. They were endowed with all those virtues which shone so conspicuously in the martyrs, namely, meekness, patience, and superhuman courage. Charity was in their heart, humility in their mind. They applied themselves before all, to model themselves on Jesus Christ, who so loved men as even to give His life for them; like Him, they forgave their enemies, and prayed for their persecutors."

Such were the martyrs of Lyons seventeen hundred years ago, and such also were the martyrs of Castelfidardo. What indescribable misery had not these latter to endure from want of proper care, until God sent them the Sisters of Charity! What inexperience in the Italian doctors who first attended them! You would see these patented executioners cutting off with scissors the mutilated fingers of the wounded, or searching with their fingers for balls in the already inflamed wounds of the sufferers; and if some indignant Catholics had not sent from Paris the large-hearted M. Léon Pagès, with a clever and devoted physician, and considerable sums of money to care for these heroic victims, scarcely one of them would have escaped death. During all these sufferings, which roused the spectators to tears of indignation, they "possessed their souls in peace," raising their hearts to God, and relishing, even to the dregs, the bitter joys of their sacrifice.

Such was the general character of the day of Castelfidardo. Its antecedents and consequences, and the details which we shall now give, regarding each of these glorious victims, will prove that we have not been guilty of exaggeration by bestowing on them the glorious title of martyrs.

General Marquis de Pimodan.

CHAPTER III
GENERAL PIMODAN

IT IS ONLY COMMON JUSTICE TO INSCRIBE at the head of this martyrology the ever-glorious name of George Pimodan. God having kept for his service in the world General de la Moricière, General Pimodan, his chief of staff and friend, was, after him, the highest in rank in the Pontifical army. He fought at Castelfidardo at the head of this phalanx of heroes, and as he was first in combat, he was the first who died on that day for the cause of Jesus Christ and His Vicar. To him, then, we give the first tear, the first page, and the first halo of glory

George de la Vallée de Rarecourt, Marquis of Pimodan, was born in 1822, of an ancient and noble house which was to be renewed in the blood of sacrifice, and whose glory (if I may so express myself), was to be regilt by the sun of Castelfidardo. Inheritor of rank and fortune, when dying at the age of thirty-eight years, he bequeathed to his son a name which the world cannot forget. *"Potius mori quam fœdari"* ("Rather die than be dishonored") was the motto of his race. He was more than faithful to it, and they could inscribe on his tomb, "Rather die than allow iniquity triumph."

It was the device of devotedness. It was in the service of Austria that he gave free scope to his military instincts, which were the ardent longings of his soul. Born a soldier, God destined him to die a soldier's death. When he learned, at the outbreak of the revolution in Austria in 1847, that he was to set out for Italy, he could scarcely restrain his delight. "Italy, Venice, Milan, Florence," wrote he to a friend, "war, glory, everything for me in these words." And, in fact, that was what he did find in this unfortunate Italy whose soil was destined to drink his blood thirteen years after. He was at Verona when the revolution of March broke out. Charged by General Ghérardi with some important dispatches for General Giulay, who was then commander at Trieste, he was arrested at Salice by the insurgents, and brought before a sort of provisional government. He advanced boldly into the room, and in a voice of thunder, demanded, "Who dared to arrest an imperial courier?" Then, profiting from the stupor which his audacity had caused, he left the hall, and stepping into his carriage, galloped away. His mission being accomplished, he returned to Terni by Venice. The day of his arrival was that of the triumph of the insurgents. Seized on board the vessel which had brought him, he was conducted before Manin. The dictator looked at him first with a puzzled countenance, as if trying to guess what brought him to Venice at such a time; then opening a drawer of gold, he stirred it with his finger, and looking fixedly at him, said: "You wish to be one of us, and to fight for the liberty of Venice." The eyes of George Pimodan flashed indignantly:

"Sir," he cried, "I am of a noble family, and an officer of the emperor's; I know my duty!" The consequence of this interview was that he was arrested; however, he again succeeded in escaping, and reached Verona, where the old Marshal Radetzky took him as his orderly officer.

At the end of the campaign he was captain of the staff; and it was to him that Radetzky entrusted the charge of bringing to Vienna the banners taken from the enemy. After the Italian campaign he made that of Hungary, where he likewise distinguished himself. Here he fell into the hands of the Hungarians, and was confined in the prison of Peterwardein. "I will not question you regarding the operations of your army," said the General who was in command of the fortress to him, "as I know you will not answer me. I could order you to be shot; but we are not savages; you shall remain here as prisoner of war. George Pimodan was not a man to accept captivity without a struggle. He tried to escape and deliver the fortress into the hands of the Imperial soldiers: cited before a council of war for this deed, he was condemned to death. Believing his hour had come, he prepared himself for death like a Christian and a soldier. On one of the panes of glass of his prison cell he wrote with his diamond ring the following simple words, which revealed his noble mind:

The eyes of George Pimodan flashed indignantly...

"Adieu, dear parents, I am going to be shot; however, I am calm and resigned; I die full of faith and hope. Dear mother, your sorrow is my only pain." Again, God, who reserved him for a more glorious death, did not accept his sacrifice. The triumphant arrival of General Haynau caused the execution to be adjourned, and he was saved. In 1855, George Pimodan, at the age of thirty-three, was lieutenant colonel. He was required to take the initiative to be raised to the rank of colonel, but the Austrian laws demanded that he should obtain from the emperor letters of naturalization, and to do so would be to renounce his title of Frenchman. M. Pimodan did not hesitate an instant between the title of Austrian colonel and that of son of France; the choice of such a heart could not be doubted; he left the Austrian service and came to live in his native country. A brilliant marriage seemed to secure the happiness of his future prospects in life; but just as he was enjoying the peace and calm of domestic life, the cry of distress from the Roman Church resounded through Europe. This painful cry re-echoed painfully in his heart, and shook to its very depths his martial and devoted soul. In one moment his resolve was made. His noble wife did not try to dissuade him from it, and in a few days he was in Rome beside General de la Moricière, who with that foresight by which friends know one another, took him into his confidence, and appointed him his chief of staff. They had not long to wait. Whilst Garibaldi was taking possession of Sicily, a troop of four hundred revolutionists crossed the frontier of Tuscany, and invaded the Papal States. They were led on by the notorious Zan bianchi, of '48 fame. These bandits expected to find a sympathizing populace, and soldiers who would allow themselves to be disarmed without a struggle; but they had reckoned without General Pimodan and the Pontifical Gendarmes. Led on by such a chief, and powerfully aided by the indignant countrymen, these brave fellows, only sixty in number, defeated the four hundred men under Zanbianchi, killing a great number, and pursuing the remainder in their shameful flight. This brilliant affair, which was known by the name of "The Battle of the Grotto," was the début in Italy of the brave Pimodan and the pontifical troops, and it proved that, incomplete as the little army of General de la Moricière was, it was fully equal to the task of defending the States of the Church against Garibaldi and his accomplices, if Piedmont had not thrown off the mask, and openly invaded the Roman States, which their treachery had failed to acquire. From June to September, General Pimodan assisted General Moricière in organizing the army, and a means of defense, and when the day of the decisive struggle came, he was there, as ever, beside his chief and his friend, ready to fight and to die for that holy cause to which he had devoted himself. The French priest, whose beautiful and interesting letter I have already alluded to, met Pimodan's column near Tolentino:

"I saw," said he to me, "the noble General seated near a table in the inn; maps were scattered around; he seemed to have no doubt regarding the issue of the struggle, and spoke to me with perfect calm, his face beaming with extraordinary brightness. He pressed my hand, saying: 'We will meet again at Loretto.' On the threshold I returned to see him once more, and left him with a broken heart."

The priest and the soldier did meet again at Loretto, on the eve of the battle. General Pimodan, mingling in the crowd of officers and soldiers, received the Sacrament of Penance, thus preparing himself for the next day's combat according to the grand Catholic and French method of the Turennes, the Condes, and all his crusading ancestors. If a passer-by had asked what this crowd dressed in uniform, which pressed round the doors of the church meant, they could be told it was an army which was confessing before being murdered for their faith. The next day, at four o'clock in the morning, kneeling beside General de la Moricière in the sanctuary of Loreto, shaded by those same walls which formerly sheltered the Mother of God, and God Himself made man. General Pimodan received the sacred body of his Savior, precious pledge of peace for the living and of salvation for the dead. Prostrate on the pavement of that temple, he prayed and meditated a long time; he gave a long last thought to his wife and children, and, undoubtedly, he offered anew his life to God for the triumph of his Church. When he arose his sacrifice was registered on high, and had been accepted by God: nothing now was wanting but the palm and the crown, and the battlefield was to give him these. A few hours later he rushed on the Piedmontese at the head of his troop, fought like a lion, actually electrified his soldiers, and astonished his enemies by his bravery. Whilst he held his ground all went well, notwithstanding the inferiority of numbers; but when he fell, all hope of success fell with him. His harangue to the Franco-Belgians before the battle was as follows:

"As for you, remember you are Frenchmen and Catholics!" As he was giving his orders from under a mulberry-tree, he received simultaneously three wounds: one in the face, one in his foot, and a mortal wound in his breast. When struck by the first ball, he cried: "Courage, my children, God is with us!" When struck by the second ball, he repeated it again, and the final blow found him still repeating the same grand words. He fainted immediately, and they took him into a neighboring cottage, where he received some attention. In the midst of his pains, the hero forgot himself to think of the success of that cause to which he had given his life. "My friends," said he to those around him, "leave me to die here, and return to your post to do your duty." General de la Moricière, knowing he was mortally wounded, went to press his hand, and say a last adieu, before setting out on his way to Ancona. Perhaps at that moment he envied his fate; for there are moments, even in the life of a hero, when he would fain lie down and die. Ah, if the king, good fellow, destined, perhaps, like the Constable of Bourbon, to end his miserable existence at Rome; if Victor Emmanuel had passed by and heard the dying moans of this new knight, "without fear or reproach," weltering in his blood, and dying on strange soil, General Pimodan could say to him in the words of Bayard: "It is not I, it is you, sire, who are to be pitied; you, who bear arms against your father, the Sovereign Pontiff, and the Holy Church, your mother." This generous defender of the Pope and Church manifested to the end the sentiments of a martyr. I shall permit the noble young man who received him in his arms, and who never left him until after his death, relate the last moments of this hero. This was Ernest Maestraeten, a student of medicine at the Catholic University of Louvain, and who during the battle had to ply the twofold calling of surgeon and sergeant, dressing the wounded and at the same time defending them, bayonet in hand:

32

"Courage, my children, God is with us!"

"The doctor and myself were just commencing to dress his wounds when our party was completely crushed by the Piedmontese, whose numbers were constantly increasing. The doctor, perceiving this, said to me: 'Maestraeten, we had better be going.' I replied that I would not leave the General nor the other wounded men; he said nothing but went away. I then remained alone with the wounded, my own leg also being somewhat injured. There were in all about thirty men, between officers and soldiers: some had their wounds dressed, others were awaiting my attention; blood was flowing on every side. It would be useless for me to describe the moans which escaped from these brave men. Our house was surrounded by the Piedmontese; and, notwithstanding the black flag which we had hoisted, they fired several shots in through the doors and windows, which, fortunately, did not do us any great harm. A Piedmontese officer came in, and we surrendered as prisoners. General Pimodan understood his position perfectly well, and awaited death with admirable calmness. He entreated of me not to leave him, to which General Cialdini consented. We then conveyed him to the Piedmontese outposts, where we were lodged in a beautiful house. General Pimodan suffered intensely, yet he bore all with the patience of a martyr; he expired about midnight."

Thus died, on the night of the 18th or 19th of September, George Pimodan, at the age of thirty-eight, leaving behind him an immortal name, and bequeathing to Catholics of all generations a sublime example. He was lamented, blessed, and glorified, by millions, who, three months before, were not aware of his existence, and whose admiring gratitude will be transmitted from age to age, ending only with the Church, that is to say, with the world. I will not speak of the deep regret which the death of George Pimodan caused in the hearts of all who knew him. Naturally chivalrous, affectionate, and kind, he endeared himself to all with whom he came in contact. His countenance was the reflex of his soul: his deep blue eyes and manly bearing had a peculiar charm. The entire body of Catholics gave to George Pimodan and his companions the glory of a splendid funeral, and from end to end of the Catholic world their glorious names resounded in the prayers and discourses which a grateful clergy and people poured forth over their tombs. The Holy Father ordered that the body of his brave General should be interred in the Church of St. Louis of France at Rome; he himself defrayed the expenses of the funeral. I shall here insert the inscription which the Sovereign Pontiff caused to be inscribed on the facade of the church:

GEORGIO DE PIMODAN,

VIRO NOBILISSIMO,

DUCI FORTISSIMO,

QUEM PRO SEDE APOSTOLICA,

MAGNÆ ANIMÆ PRODIGUM,

CATHOLICUS ORBIS LUGET.

PIUS IX. PONT. MAX.

SUO ET ROMANÆ ECCLESIÆ NOMINE,

SOLEMNE FUNUS,

TANTÆ VIRTUTI ET PIETATI DEBITUM,

MERENS PERSOLVIT.

TO

GEORGE OF PIMODAN,

A MOST NOBLE MAN,

AND MOST BRAVE GENERAL,

WHOM, WASTEFUL OF HIS GREAT LIFE

FOR THE APOSTOLIC SEE, THE CATH-

OLIC WORLD LAMENTS.

POPE PIUS THE NINTH,

IN HIS OWN NAME, AND THAT OF

THE ROMAN CHURCH,

IN GRIEF GRANTED SOLEMN FUNERAL RITES

DUE TO SUCH GREAT VIRTUE AND PIETY.

This inscription reminds one of those which the first Christians engraved on the tombs of the martyrs in the Catacombs. The words, "wasteful of his great life," are sublime. To merit such praise, and to receive it from the lips of the Vicar of Jesus Christ, is the greatest glory to which a Christian could aspire. After such an eulogium, falling from such lips, nothing need be added but to glorify God.

Mizael le Mesre de Pas.

CHAPTER IV

MIZAEL LE MESRE DE PAS

FTER THE NAME OF GENERAL PIMODAN, the next which presents itself to my pen is that of the purest and most amiable of young men, Mizael le Mesre de Pas, choice victim amongst all those who voluntarily offered themselves to God on the altar of Our Lady of Loretto. He was, perhaps, the first who thought of offering himself to the Holy Father, the first amongst the French volunteers who shed his blood for the Church, since he received the wound of which he died two days before the battle of Castelfidardo. General Moricière, who was well aware of the force of character and nobility which was hidden beneath his frail constitution, loved and regretted him in a singular manner. The history of his sacrifice and of his glory naturally comes after that of the immortal Pimodan. Born of parents who were devoted heart and soul to the Catholic faith, Mizael de Pas was always a fervent Christian. Of a naturally quick and hasty disposition, he so completely knew how to master his character, that after his death those words of the Gospel, "He was meek and humble of heart," could well be applied to him.

Those who knew him were well aware of the delicacy of feeling, gentleness of disposition, and above all the amiable modesty which ever characterized him. This reserve and mistrust of himself had nothing weak about it, as he always desired to lead a useful life. This desire was inherent in his soul, which was prepared by great examples and family traditions to expand to still nobler inspirations. Besides accepting the inheritance of birth and fortune bequeathed to him by his ancestors, he aimed at something more, something more precious still: this was to render himself worthy of the legacy of paternal virtues which they had left behind them. With this intention he embraced, while still young, the military life. In 1849 he wished to enter a celebrated preparatory school in Paris; but his mother, fearing the influence of bad advice and bad example, consulted a holy priest who knew him well. His answer was as follows: "We cannot prevent Mizael from knowing evil; his religious principles are unflinching. Evil, which he will see in all its deformity, will give him a horror of it, and his morals, notwithstanding the danger, will remain pure. Action is better for him than inaction." On hearing this his mother had no more uneasiness, this prediction, based on an absolute confidence in the energy of the noble child, was fully realized. Mizael behaved himself in so firm and simple a manner with his new companions, that in spite of the purity of his morals, which was to them a continual reproach, he was loved by all, and had not to suffer any of those trials so frequent in colleges and schools. Just as he was preparing for his examinations, about the success of which his professors were certain, he fell ill.

Three times he recommenced his studies with his wonted ardor; three times sickness came, thus destroying his future projects. These obstacles were not without a providential end, as this was the way in which God willed to try this young Christian soldier, and to prepare him for the future which awaited him, wherein all his desires were to be crowned far beyond his most sanguine expectations. Returning to his family, Mizael now a young man, sought in works of charity a remedy for the activity of his mind, and a prelude, by the sacrifice of his time and pleasures, of that which he was later to make of his life. He had a singular love for the poor, and amongst the offices of the Society of St. Vincent de Paul, of which he was an assiduous member, he had a special love for that of Ramoneur, whose duty it was to seek out the poor little children from the bosom of the deepest physical and moral misery, instruct them, patronize them, prepare them for their First Communion, by teaching them how to purify their souls in the Sacrament of Penance, their poor little souls which were sometimes as black as their faces. Mizael de Pas devoted himself to these poor abandoned creatures with touching charity, thus serving Jesus Christ in the person of His suffering members, before serving Him in the person of His representative here below by the effusion of his blood. But these pious occupations did not suffice to occupy his time sufficiently, and the thought that he was useless often threw him into great depression of spirits. He wished to enter the school of St. Cyr, or the Polytechnic School, but then his delicate health prevented him. His military vocation, being thus frustrated, left in his mind an emptiness which nothing could fill, and he expressed his sentiments with singular energy in moments of familiar intercourse. "It is very easy," he would say, with a sigh, "to tell me to do something, but what can I do? My health will not permit me to continue my military studies; I have no taste for jurisprudence or diplomacy: nothing, then, remains for me but to become a country gentleman. They say this to distract my mind and induce me to take an interest in something. Do they mean by that to have me engage myself in the married state, or devote myself to the pleasures of the chase?.... Hunting sometimes is very pleasant, but, after a day's chase, what remains? I run after my dog, which runs after a hare or rabbit; I do nothing more than he; on the contrary, without him I would have caught nothing; he knows very well how to catch game without me. No, no; I have been created for something else! The military life is the life for me. I love discipline, frank and loyal customs; to serve God and my country with all my heart; to be a good comrade; to fulfill my Christian duties without human respect; to salute the Madonna, to say nobly and simply her chaplet; to be brave on the battlefield, that's what suits me. After serving my country well, return to enjoy domestic life yes, my gray mustache will inspire confidence then, with the help of God, I will associate myself with all good works, encourage them; do as my father has done; make our good tenants comfortable; relieve the wants of the poor, reminding them that the Son of God, our Divine Redeemer, was poor like them, and became poor for their love; that the happiness of heaven awaits them, if they bear their cross with patience; exercising a moral and kind influence over all; teaching children, forming their minds and hearts to virtue such is my dream of the future! Has God given me these thoughts to renounce them? Rest before work, never, never!...." Such were the noble aspirations and regrets of Mizael de Pas, when events in Italy opened to his ardent and aspiring soul a new horizon. Since the publication of the fatal pamphlet, entitled the *Pope and the Congress*, which was

39

the first dagger plunged in the heart of the Papacy, he knew that a path of persecution had opened for the Church, and a path of sacrifices for Catholics, and hence determined on offering himself to the service of the Holy Father.

In the month of January, 1860, three months before the departure of General de la Moricière for Rome, Mizael was one day conversing with his sister, a religious of the Sacred Heart, when he said to her with the greatest calmness: "Sister, I am going to start for Rome; as yet I have not spoken of this to anyone, as I intend taking counsel before I act. Can a child of Holy Church see unmoved the affliction of the Sovereign Pontiff? What! The Father of the Universal Church is forsaken; traitors have penetrated even into his palace; he has resolved not to leave Rome, but rather to die on the tomb of the Apostles; his patience is that of a martyr. What! People hear and say these things, and yet no person arms himself for his defense! I will go and prostrate myself at the feet of His Holiness, and say to him: Most Holy Father, I offer you a devoted heart, dispose of my life and fortune as you please! I know I am good for nothing. The Holy Father will perhaps smile at me; but do you not think that in his heart he will feel consoled? He is the Vicar of Jesus Christ, and this little consolation will be to me the greatest reward. If he refuses, I will return, as I shall have done my part. If he accepts me, I will join his Guard. What an honor to draw my sword in defense of the Holy Father! Ah, my sister, if ever you hear that the sacred person of the Holy Father is attacked, be assured that your brother is no more!" A few days after his sister met him in the parlor, completely crest-fallen. "My sister," said he, "I am good for nothing; it was ambition, and a desire of being distinguished, actuated me the other day when I was speaking to you. I do not know how to content myself with the ordinary and common life. A sensible man who takes an interest in me told me it was foolishness. I insisted it was not; he persisted it was. I do not know what to do." Then rousing again, he said: "When a father is in danger, we run to help him; when a prince is attacked, we glory in defending him; and now it is the Vicar of Jesus Christ, his representative here below, and I have not yet gone to aid him. We ought not to be useless weights on the earth. My father often said that we were not created to enjoy ourselves. Someone must make a move, others will soon follow! But, no," he said, again getting grave, "we must wait and pray. Do not speak of this anymore; but pray that I may know the will of God, and be faithful to it." The admirable young man kept his resolution, and did not speak of it except to God. He increased his alms, asked the prayers of several religious communities, engaged the prayers of the little chimney-sweeps, and the numerous families whom he secretly assisted with so devoted a charity, that the Sister of Charity who had charge of that quarter called him "the hidden saint." He propagated, as far as in his power, the pastoral letters of the bishops, and all pamphlets written in defense of the Holy See.

"It is strange," he would say, "how very few have sufficient courage to follow their own convictions. Everyone trembles for his own interest, and how zealous wicked persons are to distribute their false doctrines. Are we not then obliged to do all in our power to enable the language of truth to be heard by our poor country people? To do a little good, earnestness is necessary, and how few really are in earnest; egotism vitiates everything; the least difficulty serves as an excuse. His spirits were becoming daily more depressed, and his health impaired; in vain they tried to rouse him; the holy impatience with which he longed for his sacrifice was preying on him, yet he humbly waited for God's own time. The moment came at last. On hearing the news of General de la Moricière's departure, an expression of delight beamed on his hitherto pensive features; he knew the long-wished-for hour had come to rise from his silence and obscurity, and after having invoked, in the Church of Our Lady of Victory, the aid of her to whom he had been consecrated on the day of his baptism, he went to seek his virtuous mother. "Mother," said he, "will you act my father's part towards me now?" Her eyes filled with tears; but in silence her heart had consented, and she did not even for a moment think of disputing his soul with God. She was a widow; her eldest son and daughter were married and lived far away; her second daughter had given herself to Jesus Christ; Mizael alone remained as the only consolation of her old age;

however, she hesitated not, and made, for the second time, the sacrifice, like to Abraham's, which God had demanded of her. She remembered what her pious husband often said to her:

"My daily prayer is that my children may love and serve God." She prayed, wept, pressed her son to her heart, and giving him her blessing, as Jacob did to Benjamin when departing for the land of Egypt, she allowed her beloved Mizael to set out for the Italian land, whence he was to return no more. Before his departure Mizael distributed all the money that remained to him in alms, reserving only as much as would pay his traveling expenses. His sister having expressed her fear that he was not keeping sufficient money for this purpose, he replied: "No, no; leave me to do as I like; good cannot be done without money, and money given for souls will never be missed; besides, they will pray all the more for the Church, and just now we must entreat, conjure, importune God; in a word, do Him violence, like the widow in the Gospel. Mother will send me funds to Rome, and when there, if I see the Holy Father requires money, I will ask to have my property sold. Could I make a better use of the inheritance which my good father left me? Our fortune is not our own, but a deposit entrusted to us by God." Later on:

"Oh! no! I will never have cause to regret it; God will provide for me." He said all this with a calmness and peace which had something celestial in it. He went constantly to ask prayers for the Holy Father, the Church and himself. He often said: "We begin things for God, and very often dreams of ambition and of being distinguished creep in; pray, my sister, pray that I may act for God alone." Such were the truly admirable sentiments of Mizael de Pas at the time of his departure. Like many of his companions he had a presentiment of his death. He knew well that in this great cause of the Sovereign Pontiff, Vicar of a crucified God, voluntary victims were necessary, and he went to offer himself as a holocaust. His eldest sister, foreseeing the danger, tried, when accompanying him to the railway station, to shake his resolution. "You are too weakly," she said, "ever to make a good soldier; can you not substitute in your stead some strong and experienced man? They will render far more service to the Pontifical Army."

"Sister," replied the courageous young man, "it is devoted hearts the Sovereign Pontiff needs; if I die I shall pray to God that my blood may bring blessings to my country and my family."

This was their last parting. Leaving Paris on the 3rd of May, he soon arrived at Marseilles. Just when on the point of embarking, he wrote as follows to his mother: "My eyes fill with tears every time I think this steamer will separate me far from you, and I fancy I see you still weeping; but I feel my courage revive when I think that at the other side of the Alps tears are also shed, tears which recall those shed in the Garden of Olives. My good mother bless again your son; with God's help I will not falter." Mizael arrived at Rome in the beginning of May, and when he presented himself to Cardinal Villecourt, the good old man was moved to tears at the sight of this amiable young man, so firm in his language and so simple and heroic in his devotion, and he pressed him to his heart as a child of benediction. General de la Moricière also received him with joy and kindness, and employed him almost immediately as his secretary. Mizael de Pas procured a uniform, and was one of the first volunteer guides of the Pontifical Army. I heard from a good priest who knew and loved him well, that in his inmost heart he nourished the desire of consecrating himself to God in the holy ministry, and that if he returned from Castelfidardo, he would undoubtedly have taken orders. God, in his impenetrable designs, had willed otherwise: instead of the crown awarded to a long and laborious priesthood, he reserved for him the shorter and more glorious palm of martyrdom. I have already related the circumstance of his being wounded.

It was on Sunday, the 16th of September, about eight o'clock in the evening, two days before the battle of Castelfidardo, that Captain de Palfy received orders to conduct a reconnoitering party on the Asimo road. He took with him two carabiners, and asked a volunteer for guide. Mizael had just arrived at Loretto, and although he had marched all day without breaking his fast, and was consequently greatly fatigued, yet he did not hesitate, but willingly offered to go, delighted at the thought of having at last to encounter danger. M. de Palfy set out with his little escort. Having passed the bridge of Musone,

Mizael de Pas, hit by the splinter of a bomb, had his arm
broken: at the same time his horse fell upon him...

they advanced by the high road, ignorant that two cannons were pointed at them. When they had gone about a hundred and eighty meters, two shots were fired, two or three minutes between each shot; one of the carabiners was wounded and his horse killed. Mizael de Pas, hit by the splinter of a bomb, had his arm broken; at the same time his horse fell upon him; however, he contrived to extricate himself, and dragged himself along, aided by the other carabiner, until he became powerless from loss of blood and intensity of pain. Some countrymen were called to transport him to Loretto, and there, before the almost inanimate form of the noble youth, those heartless men were not ashamed to dispute the price which they exacted for their services, as if he were a prey that had fallen into their hands. At his own request they took him to the house of the Jesuit fathers at Loretto, who received him with open arms, and showed him great charity during his stay with them. Three surgeons dressed the wound, then he was transferred to a hospital in charge of the French Sisters of Charity. There, on his bed of pain, he heard the noise of the battle of Castelfidardo, which he followed in all its phases with painful anxiety; he incessantly questioned the nuns with feverish uneasiness, and when at last he heard that the Pontifical Army was vanquished, crushed, and destroyed, he raised his eyes to heaven, exclaiming with unspeakable anguish: "What a misfortune! what a misfortune!" Then he remained plunged in a mournful silence. His soul, strong to bear up against his own sufferings, was not so against those of the Church. Shortly after he heard a great tumult; it was the wreck of the conquered army returning in disorder to Loretto. As they feared there would be an attempt at resistance made the next day, they thought it safer to transfer the wounded into the Church of the Holy House. Mizael was accordingly taken thither, about four o'clock in the evening, accompanied by the almoner; he spent two entire days praying, and reciting his chaplet continually.

With what joy must not this pious young man have tasted the first fruits of that martyrdom, which he had so long desired, in that incomparable sanctuary! With what loving eyes must he not have contemplated that humble dwelling, wherein were accomplished the greatest mysteries of our holy religion!

There the angel saluted the Virgin Mary; there the Virgin Mary conceived Jesus Christ, her Creator and her God; there the ineffable annihilation of the Incarnation commenced; there God made man grew up under the eyes of his Mother and the good St. Joseph, hidden, unknown, seemingly the last of those He had created; there He taught us to love work by working, to value obedience by obeying, to humble ourselves by his humility; in a word, there He taught us how to practice all those virtues which would render us pleasing to Him. What a spectacle for a dying Christian, for a martyr, for a crucified disciple of a crucified God! It was undoubtedly from contemplations such as these that Mizael de Pas drew that perfect faith, patience, and angelic resignation, which marked his last moments with a truly celestial character. There was something more even than resignation, there was joy. He kept constantly repeating: "How happy I am to have been the first to shed my blood for the Holy See!" He suffered a great deal; but he offered all his sufferings to God, and their bitterness was changed into delights. "Oh, how noble he was in the midst of his sufferings," wrote a French priest, who saw him the day following that on which he was wounded; "what courage, what resignation, in this pious young man!" Although suffering intense pain, the perfect serenity of his face was something angelic. To all who approached him he smiled and said: "Pray for me." He was never heard to utter a word of complaint; his only regret was to have gained his paradise so easily, having done, as he said, nothing. The day he was wounded the chaplain of the Franco-Belgians said to me:

"My good M. de Pas was the flower of my angels and brave men!" By an interposition of Providence, which people call chance, it happened that the Superioress of the Sisters of Charity at Loretto had spent several years in the house of the Sisters at Lille, which was founded by the father of Mizael de Pas; thus, the spouse of the Lord was enabled to render to the wounded and dying son in a strange land the hospitality which the father had given her five hundred leagues from there in his native town. Mizael, being told that amputation was necessary, confessed and communicated on the 18th, at six o'clock in the morning; but the operation being considered either useless or impossible, did not take place. He lived on for six days in the greatest sufferings, yet his patience did not even for one instant flag. He often said to the sister who wished to call the doctor: "Do not disturb him; I prefer you would pray for me."

The night before his death, when he saw the sister who attended him weeping, he said: "Why do you weep, sister?" "Because you are so ill," she replied. "Well," said the heroic young man, "if I die, so much the better; I am quite satisfied to go to God; I have nothing to regret; it seems to me that I am well prepared now; later on no one knows what may happen." Again, he said: "For God's glory I came, for his glory I will die." He frequently kissed a cross blessed by Pius IX, and to which was attached a plenary indulgence at the hour of death. He constantly invoked the aid of the Holy Virgin, indeed his devotion to the Mother of God had something truly filial about it, he was born on the feast of her Assumption; wounded on the feast of the Dolours; he prayed to die on the day she is invoked as Mother of Mercy. "Tomorrow will be the Feast of Our Lady of Mercy: ask this good Mother to deliver her captive," said he to the sister who attended him on the 23rd of September. The 24th he seemed better, and even dictated a letter to his mother; however, about four o'clock in the evening, as he was reading his prayer-book, his sight suddenly grew dim; he knew at once it was death, and immediately asked for the chaplain of the hospital, and, although he had communicated that morning, he requested to receive again the Holy Eucharist and Extreme Unction. Having received the last sacraments with angelic piety, he expired at eight o'clock that evening. His pure soul, having passed through the crucible of sufferings, entered joyfully into the blessed abode of the elect. Innocent victim, chosen martyr of the Church, amiable and holy Mizael, pray for us! I will not speak of the affliction of his family on hearing of his death. He was wept for by the Holy Father, who, in memory of him, bestowed on his brother, and his descendants, the title of Roman count: never was a distinction of this kind purer or more glorious in its origin. The mortal remains of Mizael de Pas, having been brought to France by his beloved brother, received singular honor in his native land. The élite of the town of Lille assisted at the obsequies celebrated for him and his companions with great fervor, and a great number of young men and notable persons of this illustrious city wished to form a cortege of honor to accompany his remains to their final resting-place in the diocese of Arras. The heart of this Christian hero, so burning with love for God and the Church, was to have been deposited, according to the wish of his brother, in the Church of Loretto, in the spot where Mizael had remained two days on his hospital bed; but, through fear of the profanations of the Revolutionists, this pious desire could not be executed, therefore, the Sisters of Charity decided on keeping this precious relic in their chapel. It is there the heart of the noble young man lies buried, awaiting the day when the Archangel's trumpet will summon it to share with his soul the happiness of the elect.

CHAPTER V

GEORGE D'HELIAND—ALFRED DE NANTEUIL— LEOPOLD DE LIPPE

OLLOWING A LOGICAL ORDER IN MY narrative, I will now speak of those young heroes who died on the battlefield of Castelfidardo; I will afterwards relate the acts of those who survived some time, but died subsequently from the effects of their wounds. Regarding several, my account must needs be very incomplete, as I wish to give nothing but positive details, therefore the history of some of these young men will be necessarily brief for want of sufficient matter; their glory, however, will not be less brilliant owing to its not being known on earth, nor will He who knows all, who rewards all, and from whose eyes nothing is hidden, refuse to crown them in their bright home above.

GEORGE D'HELIAND

God is admirable in all His ways; the designs of His justice are as adorable as those of His mercy. Whether He strikes or whether He heals; whether He leaves the dead to do His work or raises them to life again; whether He hides or manifests Himself, He disposes of all things with strength and sweetness for the greater glory of His name, and the greater good of His elect. Be it that He abandons the holy man Job to the rage of Satan, and that naked, without a home, without children, deprived of everything, he is stretched on a dunghill; be it that He gives him back health, fortune, joy, a numerous posterity, He is still the same God; He, who in the sublime familiarity of His love, the Christian people call the good God; for to those who know how to judge of things with the spirit of God His goodness appears more vividly in those trials which He sends to His most faithful friends than in the consolations which He gives them. We read in the Gospel, that our Divine Savior Jesus, being near the gates of Naim, met the funeral of a young man, who was the only son of his mother, and she was a widow. On seeing her the Lord was moved to compassion, and said: "Weep not." Then approaching, He touched the bier; those who carried it stood still, and He said: "Young man, I say to thee arise." Immediately he who was dead arose and commenced to speak. And Jesus gave him back to his mother. This is certainly a delightful spectacle, wherein God manifests Himself clearly by His power and goodness.

Well, this same God, this same Lord Jesus, the Eternal Master of life and death, has seen in our own days, in a corner of France, another widow and her only son, who loved each other tenderly. It was not necessary to do violence to the laws of nature to reunite them; the young man was full of youth and health; for eighteen years his innocence and beauty had been the sunshine of his mother's life, and while she had him she almost forgot her widowhood. Then God wished to demand from this mother a sacrifice like to Abraham's; He resolved on calling to Himself this young soul, and leaving her, whose soul was already ripened by solitude and grief, to sanctify herself by a solitude and grief still greater. He gave to the child an inspiration to sacrifice himself for his Church; and to his mother the grace to consent to it, even to desire it.

This widow was the Countess D'Heliand, and this young man was George D'Heliand, one of the martyrs of Castelfidardo. Oh! the beauty of Christian souls! Oh! the greatness of humanity, purified and regenerated by the blood of Jesus Christ crucified! In vain did the Curé of Madame D'Heliand beg of her to substitute a volunteer in place of her son, that son who was the only hope of her name, the only one who could hand down to posterity the holy traditions of his family. "Monsieur le Curé," she said, "it would not be the same thing either for him or for me; because the same loyalty would not be there."

George D'Heliand, in fact, set out; but before relating his departure, and the accomplishment of his sacrifice, I must say a few words regarding his birth, his family, and the few short years of his amiable life.

He was born at Angers, on the 25th of January, 1842. His family were illustrious in the time of the Crusades for having given several warriors to that holy and heroic enterprise, foolish in the eyes of the world, but profoundly wise in the eyes of Christians, an enterprise which was marked, as is generally the case with those things that are really blessed, by apparent defeat and loss of blood. Eight hundred years after, the new crusade, undertaken with a like issue against the Mussulmans of our own days, counted in its ranks the young descendant of the ancient Crusaders. The inheritance of faith had been transmitted to him with the name of his fathers, and the last scion of this noble and Catholic race died as became him, with his arms in his hands, mowed down in the flower of his age, on the field of honor, of the Church, and the Papacy. He was scarcely eighteen years of age when he left the pious College of Vannes; just opening into that period of existence when the carelessness of childhood, the gaiety of youth, the first joys of liberty and manly pleasures mingle so delightfully, and make of this age, especially for pure and Christian souls like George D'Heliand, the true spring-time and flower season of life. Yet it was at this very time that this child of predestination conceived and put into execution the resolution of leaving all these joys and hopes to hasten to the battlefield of faith and to the death of the martyrs. On the 3rd of July his part was taken, and after having passed in retirement and prayer the time of trial which his mother believed prudent to impose on him, he wrote to her as follows:

"I have reflected long on the answer which I am to give you to-day. It seems to me that, since you are willing to make the sacrifice, God will grant me the courage necessary to undertake this campaign. I will feel much in parting you: yes, certainly, the separation will be very painful on both sides; but if it be the will of God, as I believe it is, He will give us strength to bear the trial. I know there are a thousand chances to one that we may never meet on this side of the grave again. If I die, I hope the sufferings which I shall have endured will shorten my purgatory; and even if I return on crutches and I don't know what says to me that I shall be maimed, somehow I shall then have nothing but gain. You often told me that you preferred my salvation to everything; it seems to me that this is not a bad means of attaining it; besides the P. de B., who through delicacy of feeling did not wish to give me any counsel, told me that the only thing he would say was, that Zachary and I would be much more exposed to danger if we separated than if we remained together; hence, I have decided (if you think well of it) to set out as soon as I am better."

This permission which George asked of his mother she had already given him beforehand, since she had the super-human courage to desire this sacrifice. The only restriction which she imposed on him was that he would not allow any human thought to actuate his conduct. "If you go," said she, "do it only for God, in order to merit his love." She writes to a friend: "For nothing else save to sustain our holy religion, and the rights of the Sovereign Pontiff, have I allowed him go." So foreign was even the shadow of a political motive to her purpose, or that of her son.

George D'Heliand started with one of his German cousins, who was also his most intimate friend. Here is an extract of a letter which he wrote on the 30th of July, the eve of his depar-ture, to a holy priest, who had been his tutor:

"As Paul will be leaving in a few minutes, I do not wish to allow him to go without thanking you for your kind letter, and saying that I rely on your prayers for aid. We leave tomorrow evening at nine o'clock. My mother still continues in the same spirits; I wish God would infuse into me some of her courage, as I find the separation very hard. Perhaps it is the last time I shall ever see her or my sisters. It is, however, a consolation to me to think I am going to Rome to defend the cause of God. If I return I will bless Him; if I die there, I have full con-fidence that it will be for me a greater good. I am sending you a little offering, which you can add to the thirty francs I left you; having received some money from my relatives, to whom I came to bid adieu. I am thus enabled to make a little gift to Our Blessed Lady; would that I could give you much more! Adieu, my kind father, pray a great deal for us. I will write to you from Rome as soon as I can. I have so many faults to atone for, that I am happy at finding such a good opportunity of doing so, this is my sole motive."

Such was the humility of this pious young man of eighteen years: devotion to the Church, the desire of expiating what he called his "great faults;" behold the single and pure motive of his departure and his sacrifice. On the evening of the 31st of

July, after embracing his mother and sisters for the last time, he set out with his cousin Zachary du Reau. George D'Heliand spent the entire of this day in extreme agitation, troubled by the presentiment of the death which awaited him in Italy. He wrote several letters, in which he gave full vent to his feelings, not daring to do so with his mother and sisters, fearing it would sadden them. One of his sisters said when parting: "We will say au revoir (Goodbye, see you soon)."

He replied: "Oh, no; it will be adieu!" This bitterness of the chalice, foreseen and accepted, was wanting to none of these pure victims of Castelfidardo. I think it no offense either to Christian delicacy, or holy humility, to relate here a passage from a letter of Madame D'Heliand's, in which she speaks of the departure of her son:

"I thank you very sincerely for your kind letter to myself and George. Your prayers have certainly helped us at the moment of separation. We tried to hide our feelings, in order not to increase our mutual grief, and we embraced each other affectionately, but *reasonably.* Poor children! may God and His Holy Mother lead them safely to the foot of their throne, and we shall be well repaid for our sacrifice. It is only to give them back to Him that God has given us children. Let us redouble our prayers that all things may turn out for His glory and the salvation of souls." She writes again:

"Words cannot convey to you the extent of my sacrifice in parting with my George; every time I think of the sadness, uneasiness, physical and moral sufferings, which may be the consequence, I am bewildered. But we must seek before all things else God's holy will; therefore, I have done for Him what nought else save honor could induce me to do. I have abandoned everything to God; all I have asked is courage, and that everything that happens may be for His glory, and the salvation of my boy, whose departure I have believed to be in accordance with the manifestations of His divine will."

Truly the world, which is only a mixture of vanity and egotism, cannot understand such devotion, nor believe in such complete abnegation. It is necessary to be a Christian in order to understand the things of heaven, as it is necessary to be a Christian to accomplish them. Such was the mother George

53

D'Heliand left on the 31st of July, 1860, never to see again. He left Angers with his cousin Zachary, both feeling very much, but strong in their confidence in God, and in the protection of Our Blessed Lady, and of St. Anne, the dear and powerful patroness of Bretagne. They promised, if they're turned safe and sound from their expedition, to make a thanksgiving pilgrimage to her sanctuary. M. M. de Chalus and De Muller made the same promise: M. de Muller and Zachary were all that returned from Castelfidardo to fulfill it; the former did more, he took the habit of St. Francis at the novitiate of the Capuchin Fathers.

George and his cousin, stopping at Lyons, on Saturday, the 4th of August, received Holy Communion at the sanctuary of Our Lady of Fourvières, and arrived the next day at Marseilles. On the 6th, the steamboat "Quirinal," bore the two crusaders away to Rome, where they arrived on the 8th. They spent a week visiting the principal religious monuments of the Eternal City. Like the greater number of their comrades they obtained an audience from the Holy Father, and, more favored than many others, they had the privilege of assisting at his Mass and receiving Holy Communion from his hands: this Communion was for George D'Heliand his Viaticum. On the feast of the Assumption they repaired to the church of St. Mary Major, where the Pope officiated, and afterwards assisted with deep emotion at the blessing given by the Holy Father from the balcony of the basilica. George, in his admiration, related, "that Pius IX seemed to him to be raised in the air, his features bearing the impress of sanctity." On the 16th of August they engaged definitely, and then commenced for these brave young men the hardships and trials of the military life. Writing to his mother, George humorously describes their bed: "A bag of straw for a mattress, an imaginary pillow of the same material, two sheets that had been used only six months, the entire placed on a plank, and two trestles." On the 27th, after receiving the Apostolic Benediction, and a medal of the Immaculate Conception, they set out for the camp at Terni. The first day they went up the Tiber in a steamer, marched all the next night, and on the evening of the second day reached the camp, greatly fatigued, but healthy and full of energy. George D'Heliand bore this trial admirably. The life of the camp would have been monotonous if Piedmontese treason had not abridged the delay. Exercises, drudgery, and polishing of arms occupied the day. At eight o'clock in the evening Mgr. Sacré, the chaplain to the troops, recited the Litany of Loreto and some other prayers, to which the volunteers responded; then each retired to his tent. On Sundays an altar was arranged in the quarter reserved to the Franco-Belgians, where the chaplain said Mass; all assisted at it, the most pious having their chaplets in their hands. George was of the number. When not on duty he spent the remainder of the day visiting the neighborhood of Terni. The poor child made an ample provision of souvenirs, in case he returned home, as likewise an ample provision of merit for the great day of eternity.

About noon, on the 12th of September, General Pimodan gave orders to depart; the brave young men started in the best of spirits, knowing that they were at long-last approaching that impatiently awaited battlefield. A burning sun, followed by a frightful storm, marked the march to Spoleto. The Franco-Belgians were installed, as well as could be, in an old deserted farm-house, and lay down to sleep on their miserable straw beds dripping with rain. On the 13th, at three o'clock in the morning, they took the road to Foligno; about nine they halted and had the first good meal since they left Terni. Several confessed that evening at Foligno; George D'Heliand, being in the rear-guard, could not do so until later on, and again on the eve of the battle. It was from this little town of Foligno, over which shines like a halo the remembrance of one of those heavenly Madonnas of Raphaël, that George wrote his last letter to his mother. It breathed the same calm, energy, desire of combat, and confidence in God as usual. "Pray for me," he repeats, with unaccustomed earnestness. "I hope God will protect me. I am astonished at having traveled fifteen leagues in twenty-four hours without being more fatigued; evidently the finger of God is here!" God was there. He who is the way and the life, holding the poor child by the hand and leading him towards the day and the place where he was to consummate his sacrifice and receive his eternal recompense.

On the 14th no incident of note occurred during the march:

View from Spoleto.

that night they pitched their tents near the village of Serravalle, which is situated in the midst of the Apennines. On the 15th the tents were struck at two o'clock in the morning, and that evening they encamped at Tolentino. On the 16th they left for Macerta. After the evening call and prayers the chaplain read the letter of the Holy Father, granting a plenary indulgence at the point of death, and cries of "Long live Pio Nono!" rent the air. Captain de Charette just then arrived, bringing tidings that the Piedmontese had taken possession of Spoleto and Terni, and urging the Franco-Belgians to do their duty well. He was answered by ardent acclamations, then everyone retired to his tent and slept soundly. On the 17th, in order to avoid the Piedmontese lines, the column of General Pimodan took a winding route through the mountains. An order was given to load arms, as they thought they perceived a detachment of the enemy's troops in the plain. From the village of Monte Sancto, at the top of the Apennines, the brave volunteers of Pius IX saluted the dome of the church of Our Lady of Loretto, as the Crusaders, their forefathers, saluted from afar the holy city of Jerusalem.

That evening they encamped half way between Porto-di-Recanati and Loretto. Eight o'clock was a solemn moment for them all. These noble young men, several of whom were to die on the morrow, prayed with all the fervor of their hearts; then the commander ordered "all those who required confession to pass on to the office of the chaplain," announcing "hot work for the next day." Mgr. Sacré heard confessions all that night, and for the last time before the battle of Castelfidardo, the Franco-Belgians went to rest under their tents on the bare ground. On the 18th, a day forever immortal for the glory of the defenders of the Holy See and the shame of the Piedmontese, George D'Heliand and his cousin Zachary, not being in the same division, could only shake hands hastily before the battle. Of these two pure, loyal, and brotherly hands, one was to be cold in death before the end of that eventful day. At the very beginning of the combat George was wounded in the leg; and when one of his comrades, M. Tellier, who was witness of his death, met him in the plain, the brave young man said to him: "My wound has delayed me, so I am behind; however, I wish to reach the top of the hill." It was there that was situated the farm-house of the Cascines, remarkable for the heroic resistance of the Franco-Belgians.

Just at this moment George and his comrade saw four Piedmontese straight before them. George aimed at one, brought him down, and then stopped under the ditch to reload his gun, then he jumped on the edge of the ditch contrary to the advice of M. Tellier, who counseled him to wait until the Piedmontese had fired; that minute he received a ball in his head, drew one long sigh, and fell like a soldier. His comrade, in obedience to the orders given to the Zouaves not to remain with the wounded, rejoined his battalion, and that evening, when retreating, he found George in the same position, with a calm and smiling countenance; his brains were scattered about, and a pool of blood surrounded the immovable head of the martyr. This statement has been confirmed by M. M. du Bourg, Le Gonidec, and Muller, who saw him. Captain de Charette, on descending the hill, saw George, who was one of his party, and of whose death he was not aware. Thinking he was only wounded, he went up and asked him had he any message for his mother; but not receiving an answer, he raised him, and then perceived that life was extinct. He was obliged to abandon his remains, as well as those of his companions, to the brutal carelessness of the Piedmontese, who buried them in a common grave. But no matter where we are buried, as the poor body ere long turns into dust, in thinking of these poor young victims, it is to heaven we must look and say of them all what the mother of George D'Heliand said on hearing of the death of her beloved son: "I picture him to myself when struck by that fatal ball; his eyes, which were then shut forever to the light of this world, opened to the dazzling light of heaven. What a happy transformation!" Tears for souls such as his are vain, let us weep for those who loved them, and are left behind, still more for their wretched conquerors.

I cannot end this short notice of George D'Heliand without transcribing a passage from the funeral oration of the martyrs of Castelfidardo, preached by one of the greatest glories of the church of France, Mgr. the Bishop of Poitiers, wherein he makes allusion to him amongst them whom he had known

...he received a ball in his head, drew one
long sigh, and fell like a soldier...

and loved. The illustrious bishop raises a corner of the veil which was thrown over the sacrifice of George D'Heliand and his mother, and relates to the Catholic world some unknown and touching traits of their characters:

"The amiable and delicate youth, George D'Heliand, was the flower of the nobility as well as the model of fervor and innocence. On the eve of his departure he wrote the following words to one of his preceptors (I have related them before, but they can well bear repetition). 'We leave tomorrow evening. My mother still keeps up her courage; I wish I had as much as her. Parting will be very painful, as perhaps it will be the last time I shall see my beloved mother and sisters. It is a consolation to me to think I am going to Rome to defend the cause of God. If I return to my mother I will bless Him for it; if I die I feel that it will be for my greater good.' A few days before the battle he writes: 'If my conscience was always as pure as it is now, I would have nothing to fear. That is due to your prayers and those of my mother,' he adds. 'They say that we will soon have an engagement with the Garibaldians.' (In their honesty these young men did not think it possible they had other enemies.) 'I will ask their general to wait for a fortnight longer, in order that I may know better how to load my musket; however, if he came tomorrow, I am certain he would find no cowards. I will do what my uncle did at Quatre Bras, say a *memorare*, asking the holy Virgin to take care of me, and after that fire as many shots as I can, and receive as few as possible.'

You have heard the son speak, now listen to the mother (such monuments ought to be registered with care, and the sacred pulpit does not derogate from the holiness or dignity of its office in publishing them): 'You have had the goodness to be to my son a second father; pray then that God may grant him mercy, if anything remains for him to expiate. I have just received a letter bearing the news that he was killed on the 18th. I ought to be grateful to God for bestowing such a favor on my boy as to die for His Church, as well as for all the graces He has granted him during his short life. Happier than many mothers, I can look back on the good life of my George, and see that he has profited by the good teaching he has received from the other fathers. Since then, in order to preserve him from danger, God saw fit to take him while his soul was pure and spotless. May his holy name be blessed!

The mother who speaks thus is a widow; he whom she sacrificed to God and the Church was an only son, a fine young man of eighteen, heir to one of the finest military names of Anjou.

Such is the story of the martyrdom of George D'Heliand, and such is the crown laid on his pure and bleeding brow by the hands of the illustrious Bishop of Poitiers. May God be praised for having given to this wicked world of ours such examples, to His persecuted Church so many consolations, such sons to Christian mothers, and such mothers to those whom He has called to combat and die for Him.

ALFRED DE LA BARRE DE NANTEUIL

The history of Alfred de Nanteuil resembles that of George D'Heliand. He was scarcely twenty years of age, and, like him, had the triple crown of youth, beauty, and virtue. Like him, too, he left a happy home and brilliant prospects, to enroll himself in the Pontifical Army: only he was not an only son, and his mother was not a widow; therefore, his death would break two hearts instead of one; but these two hearts could lean on one another, and console themselves in their sorrow, that is, if parents can be ever consoled for the loss of their children.

Alfred Lawrence de la Barre de Nanteuil, was born on the 8th of August, 1839. When only two years of age he was attacked by an illness while at Paris, which brought him to death's door. Given over by the doctors, God inspired his parents with the desire of dedicating him to Our Blessed Lady, which they did at the foot of a statue to which they had great devotion. Nevertheless, as they did not wish to deprive heaven of a soul in its baptismal innocence, they asked from God the life of their child, only on condition that it would not be detrimental to his eternal salvation. Their prayer was heard, and God remembered it for them on the day of Castelfidardo. They had scarcely ended their prayer when all the symptoms of death visibly disappeared. The child fell into a peaceful slumber, and his stomach, which could retain nothing before, now retained the draughts which they gave him. The next day when the doctor came, more for the purpose of consoling the parents than attending to the patient, he was surprised to see him convalescent. Thus, by a miracle, God preserved this child of benediction for the glory of martyrdom.

It seems that, from his tenderest years, Alfred de Nanteuil had a presentiment of his destiny. He often spoke of St. Lawrence, one of his patrons, and said, smiling, that he would, like him, die a martyr. At his confirmation he chose the name of another martyr, St. Justin. He was naturally amiable, loving, patient, kind, and his generous and enthusiastic soul would have been often deceived in this world if God had not taken him to Himself.

In 1860, after having performed his Easter duty, on his return home, he went straight up to his father, and said to him: "I have just fulfilled a duty, but another remains for me to accomplish, that is, to go and defend the Holy Father." His parents assented to a resolution taken at such a time and for so good a cause, and Alfred, without losing time, commenced his preparations to depart. Before leaving his dear Bretagne and his well-beloved family, the soul of the young hero poured itself forth in a letter addressed to his uncle, and which is an admirable monument of faith, piety, heroism, and Catholic devotion; and which, I dare to affirm, will live eternally as the last will of a martyr:

"MY DEAR UNCLE,

"This letter will bring you tidings of a great decision, one which I have not arrived at lightly. Six months' reflection have only strengthened it; it is based on solid motives, faith, and my position as a gentleman. I am young, full of health and strength; will I spend my youth in indolence whilst a noble cause requires defenders? No, no; it is time to show the world that we know how to sacrifice everything for principle, and if nobility obliges me, how much more does my title of Christian. I believe in God, and will I allow his representative on earth to be insulted and outraged without going to defend him? No; I know I can commit faults for instance, not being as pious as I ought; but I am a Catholic, and my indignation can no longer tolerate the blasphemies uttered against my holy religion. God has given me life; I sacrifice it to Him; it is His, let Him take

it if He wills. He knows the motive which actuates me:
it is neither interest nor ambition, I will abandon myself
to His mercy and do my duty. But doing my duty will
cost nature something; and when, at twenty years of
age, we leave country and friends, no matter what the
cause we are going to defend may be, our hearts will
feel it, and our eyes will often fill with tears. Ah, yes! it
costs me a great deal to leave a mother who loves me
so well, poor Mary, who is still suffering, my brother,
and my poor little sisters whom I may never see again!
No matter, let nature be silent, the die is cast, duty calls
me. My God, give me strength to bear the trial.

"I will start from St. Briene on the 5th of May, stopping two days at Paris to get my passport and obtain
an audience with the Nuncio; then I will set sail for
Civita Vecchia, from whence I will, with God's help, go
and place myself under the orders of De la Moricière.
On the eve of my departure I will get a Mass said, at
which I will communicate, in order that God may bless
my undertaking. Will you unite with me? Pray for me,
that is all I ask of you.

"My dear uncle, I have one regret in leaving France,
the not being able to say farewell to you in person,
and thus being obliged to confide to the post an adieu
which will be perhaps eternal. But no matter, the sacrifice is made, and, if I am to die, we will meet where
parting comes no more. For I am not deceived; I can
say to you what I would not say to my mother. You are
a man, uncle, and can bear it. I leave France with the
presentiment that I shall never see it again; but if I die
it is a consolation to think that our dead bodies (for
I know I shall not be the only one), will be pedestals
for the re-establishment of right. Adieu.

"ALFRED DE LA BARRE DE NANTEUIL."

Tears fill the eyes in reading the last lines of this truly sublime
letter, there is devotion in all its purity, faith in all its energy,
immolation of self for the general good in all its heroic simplicity. Here are contained, in a few admirable and prophetic words,
the meaning of this Italian crusade, of this voluntary enrollment,
of this battle of Castelfidardo, this loss of blood, shed without
human hope of success. Ah! the success, like the end, was to

shed his blood, the victory was in sacrifice. Since Christ our Master, and the Master of all things, has willed to die on a cross in order to triumph over death, Christians, redeemed by His Blood and living His divine life, have not known or employed any other means to triumph in their turn over the attacks of hell: this method is sure, and has always been successful. They die, and when death does not come to them, they seek it. They say to their enemies, that is, to the enemies of God, for they have no others: "Here is our blood, drink it, we give it to you joyfully. By killing us you give us possession of heaven, and take to yourselves the possessions of earth."

Thus have the first Christians acted for three hundred years, and paganism has fallen; thus have they acted with heretics, and thus they have acted and will act in Italy until the day when the Revolution will be drowned in the blood of martyrs. God, who sees the depths of hearts, and who seems to have chosen from amongst the Franco-Belgian battalion, the most excellent and pious souls, in order to take them to Himself, found Alfred de Nanteuil pure enough to accept the offering of his blood as an agreeable sacrifice in his sight. He permitted that the dead body of the noble young man, should be one of those which would one day serve as a pedestal for the re-establishment of the rights of his representative here on earth; but before doing so, Alfred de Nanteuil had many trials to endure, and many privations to offer to God. Writing from Rome, about a month after his arrival, he says:

"An unexpected occasion having presented itself of writing to you, and for which I have long wished, I hasten to avail myself of the opportunity. How many things have happened since the happy days I spent with you. How many fatigues, deceptions, and moral sufferings, which kill far more quickly than the physical; but I had better stop, or perhaps you will think I am getting disheartened; and, far from that, the idea, or rather the principle, which guides me, is too strong to be frightened at the difficulties of a schoolboy. We have been reviewed by the Holy Father, who has given each of us a bronze medal, and addressed to us a beautiful allocation; we were so enthusiastic that we would have marched at the point of the bayonet. You cannot imagine the impression this scene has made on me; as long as I live I shall never forget it. It is not without emotion I tread this classic land living souvenir of Christianity; and if I had time, day dreams and songs would start from my pen. No; to bear arms, that is my poetry now. To give you an idea of what we endure, we are obliged to dress our own food and draw water; however, it is for God, and I am re-signed. Our life is that of a trooper; therefore our sheets are not of the finest linen, neither is our uniform of the finest cloth: we are soldiers, but soldiers of the Pope. We rise at four, then march about half a league from Rome, fasting, with our knapsacks on our backs, according to orders. In the evening, after the call, I often lean on the end of my musket, with my head on my hands, looking at the Colosseum, musing; then in spirit I fly to my beautiful France, and stay thinking of you and my family, until I feel the tears roll down my cheeks: not tears of regret, but tears of emotion, for my heart is full."

"Ah, mother," wrote he from Rome, "where are your marks of affection and maternal tenderness? Alas! they are gone from ever; nothing now but the strict orders of my chief, and, for delicacies, a large wooden bowl. But it is for the Pope, and I suffer in patience, as I can never do enough to expiate all my faults. I know where to seek strength, where alone it is to be found, therefore I am resigned."

"Do not fancy," he writes again, "that I am getting disheartened; no, I am not; the motive which actuated me in coming here is too strong to be swayed by physical sufferings."

Here is his answer to his brother, who wished to join him, and who asked his opinion and counsel on the matter:

"Notwithstanding our little trials, I am happy. The life is hard; but I am serving the Pope; what more do I want? I would advise all who can to join us, provided they are strong. As for you, my dear Augustine, remain at home; your presence is necessary for the happiness of your parents and family. Yours is certainly a generous idea; but God does not require the sacrifice; besides, our family is already represented in the Pontifical Army, and I hope that on the solemn day of battle it will be worthily represented. Remain to console poor mother, as she must be still feeling my departure. Ah, if I judge her by myself, her heart must be still bleeding; for is not the love of the son

nearest the love of the mother? Remain then, Augustine, my
beloved brother; not that I do not wish to have you with me,
God knows the contrary, and the tears which now dim my eyes
bear witness how my heart feels the advice I am now giving
you; but again, I say, stay for my love, and the happiness of
mother. Besides, there is great merit in giving up our projects,
and I know it will cost your generous heart no small struggle."

Thus did this amiable and noble young man scatter from
the lips of his brother the chalice which he drank himself
with so much courage. The affections of his heart, and his
bitter grief, did not lessen his moral or physical energy, and he
endured, with a strength of mind and body which was extraordinary, the forced marches which the Zouaves were obliged
to make from Rome to Terni, under the scorching sun of July.
He was in the rear-guard, whose duty it was to relieve those
of their comrades who sank exhausted from heat and fatigue
and put them into the waggons. On his arrival at Terni, he was
appointed corporal, a modest but much desired grade, and
which dispensed him for the future from drudgery and watching. In the course of the month of August he formed part of
the little expedition against the Italian revolutionists.

I have asked permission to cite here in its entirety a letter
full of spirit and feeling, in which the brave young man relates
this curious episode of his short military life:

"Since last I wrote to you I have had many a weary and
fatiguing hour. I have often thought of you when, straying
away for a few moments from the farm-house, I went musing
by the banks of the Tiber, in those delightful woods which
abound here. How often I have regretted my beloved mother
and my happy life at Saint Briene; but these regrets pass as
rapidly as the waters of the river, and, falling from cascade to
cascade, are lost in an abyss which I do not care to fathom. I
am happy; again I repeat I am happy, for I serve a noble cause.
We have a good many volunteers; my health is good. Here are
my reasons for being happy, as happy as it is possible to be
far away from my family and my beloved home, which otherwise I should have never left. Our commander is an excellent
man; he is a French man and a Breton, and knows how to lead
us to victory, in case we have battle; but the misfortune is, we

may never see any fire, save that of cigars. However, the other day, if we had had to deal with any but Italians, we should certainly have seen it. About eight days ago, twelve men, a sergeant, a lieutenant, and myself, set out for the purpose of making a descent on a house which was a haunt of secret societies. When we arrived on the spot, a short distance from Terni, we had a full view of the house by the light of the moon.

The lieutenant left me with four men to guard a road by which, after the attack, the fugitives were expected to pass, with orders to kill everyone. Not knowing how many were there, I lay flat in the thicket, just on the roadside, for it was as bright as day. I remained an hour and a half waiting, so I had plenty of time to think of my situation; I recommended myself to God, and waited patiently. Suddenly we heard a great discharge, then another, and then continued firing, accompanied with cries of fright and pain. An artilleryman galloped up to us at full speed, saying, 'Forward, skirmishers; help us.' We started at once, and, in the twinkling of an eye, we had crossed the fifty meters which separated us from the others. The firing still continued, but it was lessening. I was certain my comrades were defeated. When I arrived, I saw that the house was surrounded by six of our men and four gendarmes; the rest were inside binding the inhabitants, who were as gentle as lambs. The cowards! They were thirty in number, and we were only eighteen. But to continue my story regarding the firing which caused so much uneasiness: the lieutenant stopped his men about three hundred steps from the house, behind a large bush, and advancing alone, his pistol in his hand, went to the door and summoned the inhabitants three times times to surrender; on their not answering, he ordered the door to be broken in; and balls whizzed in through the windows. At last they capitulated; several trying to escape were caught. I caught one just as he was hiding himself in a bush. I presented my bayonet, calling on him to surrender, which he did; he wore an enormous Turkish vest. When the house was stormed, they found at each window loaded muskets and a great deal of ammunition. All were taken, and the most remarkable were brought under a good escort to Terni. Such was my great feat of arms, and yet I have no cross; that is not fair."

Alfred de Nanteuil seems to have known from the beginning

"Forward, skirmishers: help us."

that he was to drink to the dregs that chalice, the bitterness of which he felt so keenly: the presentiment of death never left him, even for a moment, since the day he left home. Getting into his carriage at Saint Briene, he said to his brother-in-law, pressing his hand, "They can have my body, but they will not have my soul." The days preceding the battle of Castelfidardo this dark foreboding increased, and his fine face wore an expression of sadness. He often spoke of his approaching end. On the eve of the battle, one of his comrades said to him, playfully, after dinner:

> "My dear Alfred, banish these gloomy thoughts; you will see your friends again."
>
> "My dear friend," he replied, "remember what I am going to say to you: tomorrow, at break of day, we are to give battle to the Piedmontese army, ten times stronger than ours; I am convinced we shall be crushed, for the Italians will betray us. But we must reach Ancona, the last rampart of the Sovereign Pontiff; the order of General de la Moricière is explicit. As for me, I have a presentiment of my death; to-morrow at that hour I will be a corpse."

He spoke but too truly, his prediction was verified to the letter; however, the distinctness of his presentiment did not prevent him from struggling next day with all the impetuosity of a French soldier, and fighting with a lion-like energy. One of his comrades relates the following anecdote, which showed his strength of character:

> "Just at the moment of battle, the Pontifical Army, numbering eight thousand men, had to cross a fordable river and numerous marshes. Alfred sank, and his shoes remained in the mud; he made several efforts to recover them, but without success, so he was obliged to fight barefoot amidst briers and stones; and his friend saw him fighting like a hero for two hours, and his feet bleeding. Just at the end of the battle, a few minutes before he died, he saw a Piedmontese soldier, about his own height, fall not far from him, he ran to take his boots, which he wore to the last moment."

In the heat of the battle, another of his friends, M. le Camus de Guingamp, who found himself beside him as they were ascending the heights occupied by the Piedmontese, said to him: "Well, Alfred, you are not yet wounded; away then with your forebodings." "Patience," replied Alfred, "the day is not yet over." He was not deceived, for in a few moments after he fell mortally wounded. He expired on the battlefield; and as he had from the beginning foreseen his sacrifice with a tranquil mind, so he accomplished it with a joyful heart. After the battle he was found lying on his back, with his arms extended, near the farm of Cascines; he had six wounds, four bullets, and two bayonet wounds. His parents proved themselves worthy of having given birth to such a son. Instead of murmurs, prayers of resignation and thanksgiving arose from their broken hearts. The child-birth of a martyr is as painful as any other, but more than all others it is accompanied and followed by ineffable consolations. For some days they hoped, or rather, not having received any official news of his death, they were in intense anxiety. Here are the admirable terms in which his father, who had no hope, wrote at the painful moment of their sacrifice:

> "If this ray of hope served to calm the heart of my poor wife, I would be grateful to God; but far from it; she sees him in fancy, sometimes wandering in the mountains without either food or shelter, tracked like a wild beast; sometimes mortally wounded, without care or sympathy. If she were certain of his death, she would weep over a terrible, yet consoling, truth; but the imagination of a mother is causing her fearful agony. Pray, dear friends, that our Lady of Dolours may help my poor wife, and hasten the arrival of the news which will dispel all uncertainty. As to myself, God is strengthening me, and has changed my natural love for my son into supernatural. I would not now, for the sake of keeping him a few days longer in this wicked world, dispute with him the palm of martyrdom. Nevertheless, so much pure blood having watered the patrimony of the Holy Church, we believe the days of triumph cannot be far distant. Our Lady of Dolours, in order to calm my sorrow, show me my son in glory!"

The terrible news, longed for and dreaded, came at last. The person to whom was entrusted the sad duty of bearing to Madame and Monsieur Nanteuil the doleful tidings, that their beloved Alfred son was no more, was edified at seeing so much resignation united to such grief: "Truly," she wrote, "the sight of these good parents, overwhelmed with grief, and trying mutually to sustain each other by faith, was admirable."

I think I should fail in a sacred duty if I did not reproduce here another letter written by M. de Nanteuil, after receiving the fatal communication; it is a worthy sequel of the letter written by his son regarding his sacrifice, which I have cited in the beginning:

> "My heart is broken, but not desponding. When God honors a father by giving him a martyr, who, at twenty years of age, abandons country, home, and friends, in order to embrace the rough life of a soldier, which he terminates by death, he would be unworthy of so great an honor, if he did not submissively unite in the sacrifice. From heaven our dear child encourages and helps us. He shows us the way to heaven, which he has won by his blood. Let us at least share his martyrdom by suffering with resignation. Blessed are they that mourn. Who will not understand this beatitude when contemplating such a death? More detached than ever from the things of earth, I ask God to render me worthy to join my son. Adieu! With my heart on Calvary, and my eye fixed on heaven, I will lovingly await our reunion in the bosom of God."

The noble parents of Alfred de Nanteuil hoped at first to be able to procure something which their dear son wore at the time of his death, especially his ring, scapular, or blood-stained shirt; "that shirt dyed with the blood of a martyr," as M. de Nanteuil expressed, it weeping. However, this last consolation was refused them. The Piedmontese, in their barbarous carelessness, had interred all the victims of Castelfidardo, without permitting the survivors to recognize their dead. From that day the parents of Alfred de Nanteuil have never heard anything regarding him; they have accepted this last sacrifice with that strength of mind which faith gives, and are resigned, remembering the glory which their well-beloved son enjoys in heaven, and the joy they will one day experience when meeting him there never more to part.

LEOPOLD DE LIPPE

Leopold de Lippe is another of these noble characters, and I cannot think of him without experiencing a certain emotion. I did not know him personally; but at the request of the pious and learned Curé of Ferney, his spiritual father, I wrote to General de la Moricière, strongly recommending this excellent young man, who was burning with the desire to shed his blood in the cause of the Holy See. It was, then, with deep regret I read his name on the list of killed at Castelfidardo; for, on learning he was no more, I felt I had lost a friend.

I will not relate the life of the young Christian hero, I will leave that to the good priest who recommended him to me, and who knew him from his infancy. Nothing can give an idea of the grief of this father and friend, who loved him, and who still weeps over the beloved child of his heart:

> "Of Swiss origin, but French in mind and heart, M. Leopold de Lippe completed his studies at the College of Belley, where he had enjoyed the esteem and friendship of his masters and companions by his frank, open, genial manners, but especially by his innocence and piety. I dare to say he was possessed of a delicate purity, very rare in our days, and I felt when he died, at twenty-three years of age, that no stain ever tarnished his pure soul. He was naturally poetic, and so simple-minded that he had not the least suspicion of evil; there was a candor and simplicity about him which reminded one of a flower of the warmer regions transplanted into our colder climate. Nature had for him singular attraction; he delighted in grand and beautiful scenery; he visited Switzerland and Italy; Italy! poor child! when speaking of its beauty, about two years ago, he little thought its soil was so soon to drink his blood. He confessed and communicated weekly, and he did so with a faith which shone on his features, and a simplicity which disarmed all human respect. How often in his solitary walks did not the

deserted church of some village attract his steps? How often have I not myself surprised him before the altar, where the God of the Eucharist resides, pouring out his soul in prayer, or before an altar of the Mother of God. His piety had nothing austere about it; he was a good comrade and a pleasant a companion, and he joined willingly in every recreation which his conscience did not reprove. It is easy to conceive that a mind so religiously inclined ought to feel deeply the painful situation of the common Father of all the faithful, and the dangers which threatened his power. As soon as he heard that a great number of Frenchmen had gathered round the standard of the Holy Father, he experienced with enthusiasm the contagion of their noble example, and resolved to join them. His resolution was not based on human motives, his sole aim being to devote himself to a holy cause: 'Do you think,' he asked me a few days before his departure, 'that if I die for the defense of the Church I shall be a martyr?' I responded in the affirmative, and a ray of joy beamed on his features which I shall never forget. The first days of his military apprenticeship were very trying, but he bore all with Christian heroism, without ostentation, and without complaint: he was a monk in soldier's uniform. 'Our pains are light,' he wrote, 'because we combat for a noble principle.' The desire of martyrdom already filled his soul, and he seemed to have a presentiment of it, as we find him telling his mother in one of his letters, that he is very happy, and that the one ambition of his soul is to die on the battlefield. Nothing of unusual interest occurred during the remainder of his camp life, as we may judge by what he wrote from Terni on the 20th of July: 'The receipt of a few books has been a source of great pleasure to me' (he had just received his trunk). 'The want of reading, especially on Sundays, when I had not even a prayer-book, made the time seem very long to me.' In his leisure moments he occupied himself in translating a pious Italian work. He was in the neighborhood of Terni when the unexpected order came to march against the Piedmontese. Nothing more remains to be said, except to relate the manner of his death, which I will leave to eye-witnesses."

73

"Do you think," he asked me a few days before his departure . . .

The first Christians, in order to preserve the remembrance of their martyrs, were content to obtain information by inquiries, or from pro-consular acts, or any other unstudied letters from some confessor of the faith, who had himself escaped death: this is just what I am going to do now.

M. Maurice du Bourg, one of those heroes of the Franco-Belgian corps, henceforth to be as immortal in Church history as the Theban legion, writing to his family, on the 28th of October, after a long interval of silence, says:

"Excuse me for not replying to your letter sooner; I have not had a moment to tell you of my kind friend, Leopold de Lippe, now a martyr of the faith, as he had always longed to be. On the morning of the battle, coming close to me, he said, 'I wish to die today; here is my address; if you escape, write to my mother. This address I lost, and I scarcely regret it, because on my way to Lyons I met a good lady who kindly offered to break the sad tidings to you. It appeared to me too painful to convey suddenly this terrible news. His life, since he last wrote to you, was almost the same as that of us all, save that he served us as an example. As you are already aware, we left our camp on the 12th of September, marching about ten or twelve leagues daily, which did not prevent your brave boy from carrying his knapsack, unlike others, who put them in the wagons; in the evening we were quite fatigued. Now and again I was attacked by fever, and, as my office of corporal entailed many duties, I was often helped and replaced by my dear Leopold. You will be naturally anxious to know if he communicated on the eve of the battle. Here is all I can say on the matter: we always found ourselves together at the holy table, without having made any previous arrangement; but I do not think that any of Pimodan's men could have communicated on the day or eve of the battle; for, like many others, I vainly strove to do so; however, he could have done so three or four days before at Macerta, this is all I know of your child, my kind friend, Leopold de Lippe. I will add that, on the day of the battle, we fought side by side, desiring to die together; he, it appears, was judged more worthy than I was of the crown of martyrdom, which his charitable life

75

had so well merited. I saw him fall close to me, having been struck by a ball in the head; I raised him up, but he was already with the angels. I embraced his poor bleeding form for the last time, as I was obliged to leave it in order to continue fighting."

The good M. du Bourg was mistaken in thinking that his friend had died instantaneously, as some of his companions affirm that they saw him during the combat lying against a tree, weak and exhausted from loss of blood.

In any case, here is another account, given by an ocular witness, M. Paul Saucet, when writing to his family at Nantes:

"I have had more opportunities than others, and, therefore, am enabled to give the exact account regarding this glorious and fatal day. About five o'clock on the evening of the battle, I accompanied our brave General de Pimodan; but whilst crossing the battlefield, the chief of the escort thought it well to have us rest for a while, as I was carrying on my arm a stretcher. I asked permission to visit a young man who was extended on the edge of the wood, and I recognized my dear Corporal de Lippe. I called him, but in vain; he was unconscious. I can affirm he was not dead when I left him; he was then in the power of the Piedmontese. What have they done to him? Alas! the most honorable thing we can say of them is, that they let him die, for we know with what humanity they treated their prisoners."

Such were the only accounts the mother of Leopold de Lippe could gather regarding the last moments of her son. It is probable, after the second letter we have read, that he survived his wound some hours, and that the only care the Piedmontese took of him was to inter him with the others the day after the battle of Castelfidardo. But no matter whether the way was long or short, when they at length reached the goal, and so gloriously attained the end of all human existence. We know for certain (and it is all we care to know) that the prayer of Leopold de Lippe has been heard. He died as he had wished on this sad yet glorious day, and he now enjoys the presence of that God, and the blessed company of those saints and martyrs, whom he loved while on earth, and for whose glory he so joyously shed his blood.

CHAPTER VI

ALFRED DU BEAUDIEZ—GASTON DU PLESSIS DE GRENEDAN—FLORENCE THIERRY DU FOUGERAY

MONGST ALL THESE YOUNG MAR-
tyrs of Castelfidardo, one does not really know
which is the most worthy of regret, sympathy,
and admiration; and when I study beforehand
the character of one of these amiable and valiant young men I am tempted to salute him as
the most touching and admirable of all. Such is
the picture of Alfred du Beaudiez, whose life was so pure, and
whose death was so saintly and heroic.

ALFRED DU BEAUDIEZ

Alfred du Beaudiez was born at Landernau, in Finisterre, on
the 1st of August, 1840. Six months after his birth his mother
became a widow. She left Landernau, and came to live at Saint
Paul de Leon, in order to give her six sons the advantage of a
college education. From his tenderest years Alfred manifested
remarkable sentiments of piety and docility, united to a firmness of character, which always maintained him in the right
path. According as he increased in age, the love of God and
his family increased likewise. He had a passion for drawing,
to which he devoted all his leisure hours. The noise of cities
and towns was insupportable to this simple and quiet soul; his
delight was to live in the country, where he always passed the
summer season. However, about the beginning of the year 1859,
through deference to the wishes of his mother, he gave up this
quiet life, and obtained a situation as head clerk in a tobacco
manufactory at Morlaix, about five leagues from Saint Paul. It
was with a broken heart that he bade farewell to his family
and his cherished occupations; but his grief did not prevent
him from fulfilling his new duties with all the exactitude and
energy of a Christian, and during the nine months of his stay
at Morlaix, he gained the affection, esteem, and respect, of all
who knew him. His life there was quiet and retired, limiting

his friendship to a small number of worthy persons. He took his meals at a confectioner's, with several other clerks of the town, and it often happened that on days of abstinence his only food was dry bread, notwithstanding the railleries and pity which his fidelity to the laws of the Church drew on him from his companions. On Holy Thursday he piously received the Body of our Lord Jesus Christ at the High Mass, in the midst of a large assembly of the faithful, whom he edified by his ardent piety.

On leaving the church those who did not know him asked some persons, who was that elegant young man, whose deep faith and noble simplicity they had so much admired. Shortly after, when he heard the news of the formation of a Pontifical Army, he solicited and obtained from his mother permission to send in his resignation, in order to become a soldier of Holy Church. In taking this step he was not following a natural taste, but the pure inspiration of a Catholic conscience, for the military life was repugnant to his peaceful inclinations. He had a horror of the sight of blood, and therefore never went either hunting or shooting; but, filled with an enthusiasm which youth and faith give, it cost him nothing to accomplish a duty which he considered as sacred.

To someone, who, when he was leaving, said to him that he was endangering his life, his answer was:

"Well, if I die, I shall go straight to heaven."

He said to another: "I wish to give an arm and leg for the Holy Father."

"And if God demands of you a greater sacrifice will you make it?"

"Oh, with all my heart."

Another time, alluding to his taste for drawing, he said, smiling:

"If God leaves me my right hand I shall be well satisfied." He did not start alone for Rome, one of his brothers accompanied him; but, as this noble young man has survived the battle of Castelfidardo, I will respect his Christian humility and say nothing of him.

During the two months and a half that Alfred du Beaudiez formed one of the Pontifical Army, he was a "choice soldier:"

such is the testimony given of him by his commander, M. de Becdelièvre. Cited by his chiefs as a model, he was the admiration of his brothers-in-arms, who named him "the Little Saint of the Battalion," and God alone knows how many saints there were in that noble Franco-Belgian battalion! A brave Breton peasant, who left at the same time as the two brothers, but returned from Castelfidardo with his glorious wounds and the cross of Pius IX, said, in speaking of Alfred du Beaudiez, in terms of marked admiration: "Oh! how he was loved! We often spoke of him in the hospital. What good he did in the regiment by his example! He never wished to dispense himself from any drudgery, no matter how painful." And the worthy boy adds, with touching simplicity: "I, who was accustomed to being a servant, and who loved him much, often offered to take his place, for it moved my heart to see a noble creature like him in such a position;" but he always said: "Thanks, I am a soldier, and I will do my duty as a soldier."

When Cathelineau's corps was dissolved, and united to the Franco-Belgian troops, they formed a fourth company, of which Alfred du Beaudiez was named corporal. (The unit, Crusaders of Cathelineau, was started by Henri de Cathelineau, the Grandson of Vendéen Catholic and Royal Army Generalissimo Jacques Cathelineau. The short-lived unit consisted of the first group of foreign volunteers during the Crusade of 1860. As more volunteers showed up, the unit was reorganized into the Franco-Belgian Battalion). Nothing more remains save to relate the death of this young and amiable hero. I cannot do better than reproduce the two letters addressed to his mother, one of which is from his commander, M. de Becdelièvre, the other, more detailed, from one of his friends and brothers-in-arms. In reading them we shall see, that if those who died on the battlefield of Castelfidardo were saints, there were saints, too, amongst those who survived that eventful day.

Here is the letter of M. de Becdelièvre:

"MADAM

"As chief of a regiment, a painful duty devolves upon me, that of announcing to you that our good comrade, Alfred du Beaudiez, is numbered amongst those glorious victims of Castelfidardo. If not a consolation, it will at least be an alleviation of your sorrow to hear that he died as a Christian and a hero.

"Your two sons have always been choice subjects in the battalion, and if God has deprived you of one of them, it is perhaps with a view of sending you greater consolation later on.

"You will excuse me, madam, for not having acquainted you of this sooner, but the unfortunate circumstances in which we were placed have rendered this impossible"

Here is the second letter of which I have spoken, and which I could not read without being deeply moved:

"MADAM,

"I am coming to fulfill, in your regard, a duty which the capacity of friend and brother-in-arms imposes on me, a duty which would be very painful to me if I had not to address myself to a Catholic and Christian parent; for I have to touch a still bleeding wound. I mean to speak to you of your Alfred, to whom death came on the field of honor when fighting for the noblest of causes, offering to God his blood to sustain the rights of our common Father.

"After having shed a few tears over the son whom you have so well loved, after having paid that tribute which nature so imperiously demands, I, his friend, who encountered the same dangers, and for the same cause, say to you: Christian parent, console yourself, for you have a martyr in heaven. He is happy now, very happy. He enjoys that happiness which we all desire, and which he will help us by his prayers to attain. He has only preceded us by a few short hours into that eternity which will be, sooner or later, the term of our life of exile. Oh, how I longed for that happiness which God has not deemed me yet worthy to enjoy! I only lost a few drops of blood, and I burned with the desire to shed it all for the glory of God and holy Church, represented by the successor of Peter, whom they have so unjustly stripped of his royalty. I long to tell you how noble your child was on the battlefield. Always in

"*Au revoir,* friend," said he, pressing my hand...

his rank, animating by his ardent intrepidity those who surrounded him. Twice the enemy had been driven back beyond the little house which was the center of our operations. It was when making the third charge with the bayonet, that is in the heat of the action, that he received a ball a little below the breast. His sufferings were not long; he had only time to make known to me his last thoughts, which were for God and his family. "*Au revoir,* friend," said he, pressing my hand; "tell my friends that I die a good Catholic, and that I offer my death to God for the triumph of truth on earth." Then his soul fled to receive that recompense which he so well deserved. Be pleased, relatives of a friend whom I well loved, to accept the homage of my tender sympathy. I will pray for you; in return say a little prayer for me, that I may soon be able to place myself again under the banner of the Holy Father.

"ADOLPHUS B—,"

Thus died, at twenty years of age, Alfred du Beaudiez, in the flower of his youth and devotion. His death was worthy of his life, worthy of his glorious comrades, and worthy of the crown which he enjoys with them in heaven.

COUNT GASTON DU PLESSIS DE GRENEDAN

The Count Gaston du Plessis de Grenedan offers in life and death a truly admirable type of manly energy and Christian devotion. He was one of those well-tempered souls, who by their simplicity, strength of character, deep sense of duty, and chivalrous self-denial, contrast like the offspring of another age with effeminate and corrupt generations which sixty years of revolution have made us. Before this life of thirty-two years, so pure and so courageous, so nobly spent, so heroically terminated, we are astonished, and we bow with respectful sympathy and admiration.

Gaston Francis Louis, Count of Plessis of Grénedan, was born at Rennes on the 10th of December, 1828, of a family in which faith and honor were hereditary. His generation was worthy of its ancestors, as it gave to the church a priest, a nun, and a martyr. Gaston grew up in a healthy and pure atmosphere.

82

He was favored by nature, under the influence of which, along with strong grace and a thoroughly Christian education, his body and mind developed themselves with equal energy. At twenty years of age he was already what many others never become, a man.

The revolution of 1848 surprised him whilst pursuing his studies of law at Rennes, and then came the days of June, when he preluded, by a first campaign against Socialism, his first act of devotion to that great and holy enterprise in defense of which he was one day to give his life! He started from Rennes, accompanied by some other young volunteers, in order to sustain the social order so gravely threatened in Paris, and then, with a glance of his eye, he measured the extent of the evil which the entire of society was to suffer. One of those who accompanied him on this rapid expedition remembers yet with what persistent preoccupation the noble young man conversed with him, during the journey, on the near dangers which the Revolution was reserving for the venerated Pontiff, and for whom he was, twelve years later, to shed the last drop of his blood. On his return to Rennes, he continued his studies, leading at the same time the life of a perfect Christian, and on the 22nd May, 1852, he was brilliantly received as Doctor of Law. He came to Paris in 1854, with the desire and hope of becoming a member of the State Council; but, at the end of a few months, disheartened by the long waiting and the uncertainty of success, he gave up Paris and his projects and came to dwell with his family in dear Bretagne. A great and laborious undertaking was not long in preventing him from beginning that peaceful life, the delight of which he had just begun to taste.

His father, who had always great taste for agricultural works, had just undertaken an immense one in Finisterre, in the Commons of Combrit and Cléder. Already weakened by the excessive fatigues attendant on this enterprise, M. du Plessis succumbed almost suddenly to an attack of inflammation of the lungs, dying in the arms of his dear Gaston on the 13th of March, 1855.

The noble young man found himself by this fatal event head of the family, and entrusted alone with the direction of a difficult enterprise. He undertook all with a generosity of heart, accepted with energy this great duty and heavy responsibility. He immediately sacrificed all his projects, pleasures, and inclinations, to devote himself entirely to the achievement of his father's work. Far from his friends and family, whom he loved, he lived for four years, laborious and isolated in the midst of marshes with his workmen, whom he directed with unceasing activity, uniting firmness, which made him respected and obeyed, with kindness, which made him loved. On Sundays, after the holy offices of the day, he scarcely granted himself a few hours' recreation with the amiable family of the Parcevaux, who gave to the church a soldier and a martyr, and to him a companion-in-arms and in glory. It was not until the end of the year 1859, that Gaston du Plessis left the marshes, which were transformed, thanks to his care and labor, into admirable fields and luxuriant prairies. He had given a great example, rendered great service to agriculture and science, and increased the fortunes of his sisters. The first part of his existence was ended, and it seemed that the time of rest and recompense had come.

Rest and recompense were near at hand, but it was not in this world he was to find either. Scarcely had he returned home than the fatal pamphlet, *The Pope and the Congress*, which struck the Church in the face and all Catholics in their hearts, appeared. To the agonizing cry of this immortal mother responded the indignant and loving cry of her children, and the noble, Catholic, monarchical, and soldierly people of Bretagne, were the first to start for the defense of the Sovereign Pontiff.

In the month of May, 1860, Gaston du Plessis wished to set out for the Pontifical Army, and if he renounced it first, it was only in deference to the earnest entreaties of his mother, who urged that his position as head of the family obliged him to remain at home. Besides, a brilliant marriage awaited him, the preliminary overtures had been favorably received, and in the beginning of June, Gaston left for Paris in the hope of concluding his project. Then, embracing him with affectionate tenderness, little did his poor mother think she was never again to see him in this world.

At Paris Gaston met some compatriots who were preparing to start for Rome. Immediately his instincts of devotion awoke again, and he grew indignant at the thought that he was going to rest in idleness, whilst so many others were going to fight and die for the Church; and renouncing all his plans and hopes, he sacrificed once again happiness to duty, and hastened to enroll himself in the Pontifical Army. Mysterious attraction of a holy and hated cause for noble hearts! It is sufficient to have them hear of it in order to devote themselves entirely thereto. On the 30th of June, Gaston du Plessis started for Italy, after announcing his resolution to his mother by the following letter:

"PARIS, *20th June,* 1860.

"MY DEAR MOTHER,

"If you had less faith, I would hesitate to make known to you the resolution which I have taken within the last week. I came to Paris with the intention of being married, but meeting some Bretons who had just arrived from Rome, having been sent by the Pope to look for some devoted men, they asked me if I would consent to make one of a French regiment, who would bear the cross on their breast, and on their banner the image of the holy Virgin. Such a proposition has completely seduced me. I thought religion had the first claim on me; and that during my absence, which will not be longer than six months, God will watch over you all. This step has cost me something, especially when I thought of the grief you would feel; but God, who gave me the courage to take it, will give you also the grace not only to be resigned, but even to approve of it. I hope all will be over in six months, and that I will be able to return to you about January. Tell my sisters, in whose prayers I have great confidence, to make a novena for me with you and the nuns, asking that I may return safe and sound after having well fulfilled my duty. Will you also, dear mother, get a Mass said for me at Plessis for the same intention. At Marseilles the Bretons intend to make a pilgrimage to Our Lady of La Garde; I will see our good Abbé, who, I hope, will not excommunicate me. The Bishop of Guimper has fully approved of my step. He said he did not wish to urge me, but that since my resolution was taken, not only would he not deter me, but that he even thought it singular, having regard to the antecedents of our family, that they had

not been represented in this crusade, adding, that if
you were too good a mother not to feel afflicted at my
departure, on the other hand you had too much faith
not to approve of it. I have preferred writing to you
in order to avoid those adieux, which are very painful
to those who love each other dearly."

Thus, Gaston du Plessis, aged thirty-two, hastened, without
almost giving himself time to breathe, from one step to another
more complete and admirable, and at the very moment he was
about to enjoy that rest of body and mind, which he had so
well earned in the bosom of his family, from whom he was so
long severed, on the eve of contracting an alliance which was
to be the crown and joy of his noble existence, he abandoned
the joys of the present and the hopes of the future, to go far
from his native country to don the uniform of a simple soldier.
It is true it was the uniform of the Pontifical Zouaves, the glorious livery of the defenders of the Church, and for many it
was to be the livery of a martyr!

Gaston embraced his new life with the same ardor, the same
physical and moral energy as he did the first; and as he had
been a perfect student, a perfect agriculturist, he was, from the
very first, a perfect soldier. Reassured regarding the sentiments
of his mother, who, notwithstanding her broken heart, found in
her faith strength to support, and even applaud, the departure
of her dear son, he gave himself up entirely to his new duties,
and according to the testimony of one of his comrades, from
his arrival in the Zouaves, up to his death, "he lived as a saint
and spoke as an apostle." There, as every where, he knew how
to make himself loved and respected by all, always preserving
the same evenness of character and vivacity of mind, rendering
to all, without distinction, every service in his power, pressing,
with cordiality, all those generous and devoted hands which
surrounded him, bestowing his most intimate friendship on elevated and upright sentiments without regarding the inferiority
of their social condition, inviting those young men to dine with
him whom he thought in embarrassed circumstances, defending
and protecting against the hardships of military instructions
those of the volunteers who were disconcerted with proceed-
ings to which they were so little accustomed, and delighted

with the help which was lent them with as much dignity of manner as nobility of language. Always full of courage, and devoted to the cause which he had come to defend, Gaston did not hide the gravity and dangers of the situation in which he found himself. In his last letter to his mother he did not even allude to those dark presentiments which overshadowed him; but, in writing to his friends, he did not maintain the same reserve, as we shall see by the following letter:

"THE CAMP AT TERNI,
10th September, 1860.

"MY DEAR FRIEND,

"I am writing to you from our camp at Terni, where we sleep on the earth beneath a starry sky, notwith-standing which we are all well and gay, awaiting, with impatience, the moment of action. After the dissolu-tion of M. de Cathelineau's corps, we joined the Pon-tifical skirmishers. We are all full of courage and ardor, and delighted that we came. We will probably change our quarters one of these days, so that I do not know where we may be in a week. I think that God, for whom I have not hesitated to sacrifice myself in coming here, will watch over and protect my mother, and fill my place to her and my sisters in case any evil should befall me. As I always try to keep myself ready to appear before God as well as I can, I have no fear of death. If it pleases Him that I should return again to my dear Bretagne, and press once more to my heart my relatives and friends, I shall have the sat-isfaction of having fulfilled my duty in coming here to defend religion, and it will be the greatest consolation of my after life."

This was the last letter of Gaston du Plessis, the last out-pouring of this firm, calm, and pure soul. Eight days later he marched to battle with a calm brow, a tranquil conscience, and his heart inflamed with love for Jesus Christ, whom he had just received in the Holy Eucharist; and on the evening of that day he was neither amongst the prisoners at Loretto nor the wounded at Castelfidardo; for his body was stretched cold and lifeless on the battlefield, and his soul was with its

God. Madame du Plessis was a long time without hearing any tidings of her dear and noble son, during which time she was a prey to intense anxiety of mind. She could not even learn the precise manner of his death, whether he had died instantly or survived his wounds a few moments. Amongst several contradictory accounts, M. de Couessin, a friend and comrade of Gaston's wrote to her: "I had just been made prisoner, and as I was crossing the battlefield under the escort of our conquerors, with several of my comrades, one of them, M. de Perrodil, said to me: 'Look at poor Du Plessis.' I looked, and there I saw your poor son; a ball had struck him in the temple, so that death must have been immediate. He was one of those who were foremost in attacking the enemy."

Thus died Gaston du Plessis at thirty-two years of age, worthy of compassion according to human views, worthy of envy according to divine hopes: he had lived as a gentleman and a Christian, and he died a martyr. May God send to our country characters of this stamp, souls of his virtue, men of his valor, and France will be saved.

FLORENCE THIERRY DU FOUGERAY

Florence Thierry du Fougeray was, like Gaston du Plessis, a child of Bretagne. He was born on the 24th November, 1839, at St. Malo, of a highly respectable family. He was educated at Rennes, in the Seminary of St. Vincent. From his childhood he evinced a friendliness and amiability which caused him to be loved by masters and scholars. A modest and delicate reserve, united to a thoughtful mind, completed his character. His religious life was based on a deep and sincere faith, and in his piety, as well as in all his conduct, there was more of solidity than order. In him everything gave promise that he would prove to be a man of will and duty. At the end of his studies he returned to his family, and was leading a happy and peaceful life, not having yet decided what path he would follow, when God inspired him with the thought of joining the Pontifical Army. His decision was quickly taken, and he left family, friends, country, and wealth for what he considered his duty, devoting himself more through conviction than enthusiasm.

"Look at poor Du Plessis."

Florence Thierry du Fougeray.

The sacrifice was painful both to the young man himself and to his parents, for he was their only son, but on their part as well as on his, it was generous and entire. Florence Thierry du Fougeray left Rennes on the 12th of August, and in less than six weeks after he fell, mortally wounded, at Castelfidardo. One of his brothers in arms relates that the young volunteer showed himself during the days preceding the battle full of piety and courage; like the greater number of his comrades, he communicated in order to prepare for the great struggle, and a few words which he said just then seemed to indicate that he had a presentiment of his death. We cannot say at what particular stage of the battle he fell, but one of his companions affirms to have seen him in the middle of the day lying in the ditch, pierced with three balls, one in his arm and two in his body. The dying hero could only press the hand of his friend, who was going away. Nothing more has been heard of him since. When the news of his death reached Rennes, those who had known and loved him were moved with regret and admiration. A solemn service was celebrated for the soul of the brave Pontifical Volunteer in the church of St. Vincent's Seminary, where he had been educated.

At the end of Mass the Archbishop of Rennes, who was present at the ceremony, could not contain his grief, and giving vent to the sorrow which filled his truly paternal heart at the remembrance of this amiable young man, who had been for ten years the child of his love, and on whose brow he had so many times caused to descend, with the pardon which purifies, all the benedictions of heaven. "It was from my arms," said he, in a voice choked with sobs, "that he tore himself away to hasten to Rome, notwithstanding the efforts (pardon to-day the avowal of my weakness) I made to retain him."

Happy young man for not having listened this once to a voice which he was wont to revere as that of a father's. He has given his blood for the holiest cause, and exchanged the perishable crown of earthly glory for the glorious and immortal crown of a martyr!

CHAPTER VII

GEORGE MIYONNET—RAOUL DU MANOIR— JOSEPH BLANC—FELIX DE MONTRAVEL

GEORGE MIYONNET

GEORGE MIYONNET WAS ONE OF THE youngest and purest victims of the day of Castelfidardo. He was scarcely seventeen years, and had but just finished his studies when he resolved to start for Rome, and offer to the Holy Father the first-fruits of his youth. "I do not aim at commanding others, but I do aim at being a good Roman soldier, and knowing how to die, if necessary, for a holy cause." The noble child little dreamed that to know how to die, and to die at seventeen years of age, is a higher pretension than to command men; but he knew that devotion was the mainspring of his sacrifice, and he did not take pride in it even for an instant. Such is the fruit of Christian education in generous souls, and of them we may truly say with the poet:

"In high-born souls Valor awaits not the flight of years"

George Miyonnet was born at Angers, in 1843, of one of the most honorable families of that great city. He was educated in St. Paul's de Maulevrier, and in that pious retreat his precious gifts of nature and grace were quickly developed. He was already a formed man at an age when others are mere youths. Devotedness was inherent in his generous nature, and before ever he thought of enrolling himself in the Pontifical Army, and giving his heart's blood in defense of the truth, he had resolved on consecrating his life to God in the priesthood. "I believe that God calls me to a life of abnegation and sacrifice," wrote he to his sister, who was the confidante of all his thoughts: "I must obey Him. It will be very painful to me to say adieu to all, and especially to you who have been a sharer in all my joys and sorrows. But let us have faith and hope, two things which lighten every pain, and which, after a few years, will reunite us forever." He sighed for the hour of sacrifice. "When," he would often say, "shall I have the happiness of taking the religious habit?" His father, who was generous like himself, had at length consented to allow him to follow his vocation, when the events in Italy suddenly changed the plans of George. He resolved to start for Rome, in order to join the Franco-Belgian Corps, and if he arrived rather late, it was owing to his awaiting the consent of his father, who wished to try if his resolution was steadfast. He knew well how to repair lost time, and he gloriously entered heaven on the day of the battle of Castelfidardo, thus justifying those mysterious words of the Gospel, "that the last shall be first and the first last." His father relates the most remarkable circumstances regarding the departure and short military career of this heroic young man, which I shall reproduce here. This letter is addressed to the Superior of the house at Maulevrier, and is admirable for the Catholic spirit which pervades it; it reveals the greatness of the soul of him who wrote it, as well as that of the generous soul whose sacrifice it relates:

"ANGERS,
"29th October.

"MY VERY DEAR ABBÉ,

"Since George left you, I have no doubt you have been anxious to know what has become of him, in order to give some news of him to his dear companions. You formed a correct estimate of the heart of this child, when in one of your letters, about two years ago, you said: 'Your son George has a heart; he will be a man.' He has just given proof of it on the battlefield of Castelfidardo. To you, dear Abbé, a part of his glory is due, because it is you who trained him. I learned with happiness that George had fulfilled the promise which he made me on the feast of the Assumption, when, after having communicated, he read a letter received from Paris, couched in the following terms: If your son, who presented himself about two months ago, still perseveres in his intention of leaving for Rome, let him be here the day after tomorrow. The Communion, which he had that day received, rendered him firm in his answer: 'I will start,' he said; 'I have no pretensions of

93

one day commanding others, but I do aim at being a good Roman soldier, and knowing how to die, if necessary, for a holy cause.' His physical strength responded to the aspirations of his heart; his legs of seventeen never bent under the weight of his knapsack and heavy armor. He knew perfectly how to use his bayonet, and in the house of Castelfidardo he struggled as nobly as his comrades. What has become of our dear child since then? We know not. Is he still alive, fighting against those sufferings which are the disgrace of the Piedmontese? If this be the case, pray, dear Abbé, and ask his companions to pray, that God may spare him to us. Is he in heaven, enjoying the recompense of his devotion? If so, dear Abbé, share our happiness, and mingle your tears with those of his mother, his sisters, and brother.

"AUGUSTINE MIYONNET."

When writing this letter, worthy of the father of a martyr, M. Miyonnet was still in doubt as to the fate of his son, and had, therefore, some hope of seeing him again. This hope has now gone forever, and the accounts which time has confirmed, prove that George Miyonnet did not survive the day of Castelfidardo.

The following is the account of several of his comrades:

He was shut up with them in the farm-house of Cascines, where he fought bravely until the end. When, in order to save their wounded from being burned alive, these heroic young men capitulated, George Miyonnet was still standing in the first rank. At the moment of capitulation the firing ceased, the doors of the farm-house were opened, and the Piedmontese rushed in; then several of these wretches, excited, no doubt, as well as furious at the long resistance of the Pontificals, and forgetting that they had no longer before them enemies, but prisoners of war, fired about a dozen shots, which, fortunately, did not make many victims. One of these shots, more fatal than the others, struck young Miyonnet, for his comrades saw him fall, and, later on, when they were permitted to recognize one another, he was not to be found amongst the wounded.

It is, then, a fact that this noble young man was assassinated at the door of the farmstead, which was the glorious theater

One of these shots, more fatal than the
others, struck young Miyonnet.

of the Pontifical Zouaves, and his death, more than that of his comrades, was the result of an odious violation of the rights of nations, and the laws of military honor. Was his body buried under the smoking ruins of the farm of Cascines, or was it thrown into the common ditch, where the Piedmontese heaped the mortal remains of their victims? We do not know, and it matters little. All we care to know, and which we do know with the certainty of faith is, that his soul is in heaven, crowned with happiness and glory, in the society of all those martyrs, who have known, like him, from the beginning of the world, how to die for a holy cause the cause of justice and truth.

RAOUL DU MANOIR

Raoul Felix le Chanoine, Baron of Manoir, born at Troyes, on the 13th of December, 1839, was descended from a noble and ancient family of Champagne. His grandfather, who was superior officer under the Empire, was killed at Waterloo. By his mother he was descended from the great and illustrious family of Fontenoy, which had watered with its blood the battlefields of royalist and Catholic France under the Convention. In giving his life's blood on the battlefield of Castelfidardo for the holiest of causes, the young and worthy descendant of heroes did but imitate his forefathers, nay more, he surpassed them. He was an only son, and from his childhood manifested a marked vocation for the military life. He had the bearing, gaiety, courage, and bravery of a soldier, and all the efforts of his parents to root out these irresistible inclinations failed. Passionately fond of horses, it was the cavalry he aimed at joining, as we shall see by the answer he one day gave his mother, when asked what division he proposed to engage in, and which shows the sentiments which animated him, and his admiration of the military glory of his grandfather: "In what corps could a Manoir engage in if not in the 1st Lancers?" This was the regiment of his grandfather at Waterloo. Raoul was then about eighteen years of age, and his frightened parents tried again to change his resolution, or at least to delay its execution. With this intention, profiting by his passion for horses, they proposed to him to present himself at the imperial studs, advising him for this purpose to take a trip to

Montier en Der. The young Manoir, still firm in his intention, accepted this proposition only with the design of perfecting himself in horsemanship. He visited the studs at Montier en Der, and whilst there, an occasion presented itself unexpectedly, which showed the indomitable energy of his character. It was the time of races; competition was therefore open, a riding-whip being the prize, but the horse to be ridden was both restive and vicious. Caring little for the prize, but coveting the struggle and the victory over a courser reputed as incorrigible, Raoul du Manoir caused his name to be inscribed on the list. The evening before the races, when trying the terrible animal, he was thrown off and his wrist much hurt; but, notwithstanding his youth, he was not one to be frightened by such an accident, and although counseled to give up so perilous a struggle, he persisted.

The next day the race-course of Montier en Der resounded with the acclamations of a crowd of spectators, when young Manoir, mounted on the now obedient animal, outstripped his competitors, and won the victory. I may be wrong, but I fancy the struggle of young Alexander against Bucephalus, which has for two thousand years excited the admiration of the classical world, was not more perilous or meritorious than this. On his return to Paris, Raoul's only answer to his friends who congratulated him on his victory, was a smile, and the following words: "Do not call this amusement a victory; reserve that word for the future." It is certain he had in him the materials for a hero, but God destined him for better things. He wished him to be a martyr. Raoul du Manoir had decided on embracing the military career, but fearing the idleness of the garrison life, he only awaited a favorable opportunity. Divine Providence, who reserved for Himself this noble soul, was not long in furnishing one. The news of the formation of the Pontifical Army, to defend the Holy See, re-echoed in the heart of Raoul du Manoir, as it did in that of many other noble young men; his vocation had found an admirable issue; his battlefield appeared to him grander than anything he had ever dreamed of. He did not hesitate, and stifling in the depths of his heart the tears which accompanied so great a sacrifice, be resolved to start. Another young man, like him of noble race and heart, the friend

...the race-course of Montier en Der resounded with
the acclamations of a crowd of spectators...

of his childhood, and his cousin, German, ardently longed to accompany him in this holy expedition; but detained by important business, he begged of Raoul to defer his departure to the month of September, as he would be then free, and would go with him to defend the Holy See. "The month of September will be too late," prophetically replied the young crusader; "all will be over then;" and pressing with emotion the hand of his cousin, he said: "Adieu, dear Felix, I will start at once, and alone."

I will not relate the feelings of his parents, when the hour of separation came. Their courage failed when pressing to their hearts and covering with kisses their only and magnanimous child; however, they expected to see him again. Like Abraham, they preserved a secret hope that God would not accept their sacrifice, and that their well-beloved Isaac would not be taken from them. As to him whom God called, and whom the virtue of his sacrifice seemed to have already transfigured, with a heart joyful and broken at the same time; it was pain which was portrayed on his features; it was not the firmness of an unshaken resolution; but it was the deep feeling of sadness and dejection of a manly heart, which feels itself called and retained at the same time, and which understands and measures on the one side the extent of its duties, and on the other that of its strength and sacrifice.

From his arrival he proved by a magnanimous resolution, taken with simplicity and without hesitation, that he had not come to Rome to satisfy his taste, but to sacrifice himself to an austere duty. The military life which he had always longed for was an appointment in the cavalry; the handling of muskets, marching, and the evolutions of foot soldiers were foreign to his nature. Yet, however, he engaged in the Pontifical Skirmishers. A counsel, a word from Mgr. Merode had sufficed to make him accomplish this very hard sacrifice, and this word was, "The corps on which we depend most is that of the skirmishers."

"Notwithstanding my firm resolution to serve only in the cavalry," he writes from Rome on the 14th of July, "I am but a bad trooper, a so-called Pontifical Skirmisher. I have not entered the light cavalry, acting on the advice of Mgr. de Merode, and afterwards on my own convictions. The skirmishers form the élite of a choice corps. When entering this division, I had to pay a stake of 55 francs. We maneuver already as well as the oldest of the old; and when the people see us passing with our arms and baggage, ascending and descending at the gallop, covered with perspiration, they cry out, 'What a brave little battalion!' And well could they say so without flattery, for it was true. Night or day, at any hour, we would be ready in five minutes to charge the enemy. We are at present in Rome, but perhaps tomorrow, or even this evening, we may be elsewhere. Fatigue is unknown amongst us. Whenever we have a moment we sleep, having either the ground or some straw for a mattress, and our musket for a bolster."

Remembering that the next day would be his mother's feast, he finishes his letter as follows:

"Dear and good mother, tomorrow will be your feast. I am too far away to embrace you, but I will send you something which will make up for it, the blessing of the Holy Father, which I have received, so to speak, in the nick of time. Last evening eighteen of us had an audience at the Vatican, when the Holy Father gave each of us a medal and his blessing, telling us to send it to our parents in our first letter; so, dear mother, the three of us, father, mother, and son, have received the papal benediction for your feast. Is not this a pretty bouquet to give you?" It was thus that in this rare nature, embellished by divine grace and perfected by self-devotion, the tenderest delicacy of heart was united to high spirits and energy of character. The thought that he was fulfilling a sacred duty, by renouncing all his military dreams of the future, brought untold peace to his heart. Neither the forced marches, the encampments in the open air, nor the many fatigues and privations, which preluded the bloody consummation of the sacrifice, could draw from him the slightest complaint or regret. He never lost the merriment and charming gaiety which rendered him so pleasing to all his friends.

"Dear mother," he writes from Terni, on the 4th of September, in his last letter, "perhaps you will be scarcely able to read this epistle, owing to my want of writing materials. I am stretched flat, the end of my musket serving as a table, so you see my desk is not the grandest. I have just adjusted an

old pen in a piece of reed, and I spit into an old bottle where
there may have been ink about half a century ago, in order
to compose some sort of liquid which will be more or less
black when dry, which proves that, though I may be actuated
by the best of intentions, it is not often positively convenient
to send you news. All my comrades, equals and superiors, are
very well. I am on very good terms with Villele: he has been
made corporal within these few days. My turn for promotion
will probably come also; but I do not ask anything, as I am
very well as a simple private; however, I will not refuse the lace
nor the epaulets. My health is very good; I eat as much as four,
drink as much as six, and work as much as twenty."

This apparent careless gaiety was in reality magnanimity, his
motive being to encourage his parents and scatter from their
minds the dark forebodings that filled his own. Like the greater
number of his companions in martyrdom, he most certainly
had a clear and prophetic prevision of his approaching death;
and this thought, which he controlled by his natural strength
of will, was not the less vividly present to his mind. "Do you
know, Raoul," said one of his friends to him, a few days before
his departure, "the danger you are about exposing yourself to?"
"I know it very well," he replied, "and I hear an interior voice
telling me that I shall never return."

The day of Castelfidardo, which will be immortal in history,
to the disgrace of its pretended victors and the glory of its
martyrs, realized this presentiment. By the liveliness of his
faith, which was as deep and simple as that of a child, by the
rare goodness of his soul, Raoul du Manoir, absolved from his
faults, fortified by the sacraments of the Church, was ready to
appear before God, and worthy to die for Him.

In the first rank of this heroic phalanx of young men, this
handful of volunteers who have been so deservedly entitled
"the brave little battalion," he saw fall successively around him
his comrades and his friends. The battle, or rather the assassination, had lasted four hours, and he was still standing, covered with blood and black with powder, fighting like a lion,
and instead of victory seeming to seek for death. Either by
chance, or the general movement of the battle, or the huge
gaps made by the balls of the enemy, or in consequence of

...the Pontifical Zouaves found themselves gathered
into little groups of about four or five men each...

the tactics ordered by General de la Moricière, the Pontifical Zouaves found themselves gathered into little groups of
about four or five men each, sustaining one another, and thus
opposing a greater body of resistance to the attacks of the
enemy than if each soldier were given over to the ill-directed
impulse of his own courage. Raoul du Manoir, young Merle,
and M. Alain de Charette formed one of these groups, which
was already much reduced by the Piedmontese grapeshot. Suddenly, and at the same time as an order to charge with the
bayonet, came a frightful discharge of musketry from the enemy's ranks, spreading everywhere death and confusion. Messieurs Merle and Charette were suddenly separated, and could
not see or meet each other again until the end of the battle.
They were safe and sound, and their first thought was to look
everywhere for their brother-in-arms, Raoul du Manoir; they
called him loudly, but in vain. They asked some comrades, who,
like them, had escaped from the general massacre, but Raoul
had disappeared; no person had seen him either amongst the
living, wounded, prisoners, or dead since the extermination of
the little army of the Holy Father. It was only the next day that
a young Pontifical Zouave, M. de Montargé, who was wounded
himself in the leg, and who had seen Raoul du Manoir fall a
few paces from him, made known his fate to young Merle at
the hospital of Osima, where the latter had called to see him.

The heroic young man had fallen dead, like his grandfather,
on the battlefield of the new Waterloo, the Waterloo by the law
of nations and European honor. A ball through the head had
deprived him of life, without changing the serenity of his noble
and beautiful face; and his soul, torn violently from his body,
entered with a bound into a glorious eternity. During forty-five
days his parents were ignorant of his fate, forty-five days of
painful suspense! All the accounts they received were contradictory. Wholly resigned to the will of God, without ceasing
entirely to hope for the return of her son, Madame du Manoir
fixed for herself the term of expectation, and to the friends who
tried to represent to her as probable the return of her only and
well-beloved son, she answered: "I will expect him until midday
on the 1st of November; if he is not in my arms by that time,
he will be where, perhaps, he is already, in the bosom of God."

By a strange coincidence, which worldly people call chance, but which Christian souls attribute to the intervention of Providence, a letter came to Madame du Manoir at midday on the 1st of November. "This is the answer of God," said she, before opening it; "Raoul is dead, he is a martyr, he is in heaven!" It was, in fact, the answer of God; and this letter, written by Madame de Rohan Chabot, announced to Monsieur and Madame du Manoir the death of their son on the battlefield of Castelfidardo. They had made their sacrifice beforehand, and they bore their great grief with that strength of mind which became the parents of a martyr. The heart of a Christian is broken and torn like that of other men, but from its open wounds escape, instead of murmurings and complaints, sublime prayers of resignation and love. One of Raoul's comrades, M. Merle, when passing through Paris on his way home, called to see Monsieur and Madame du Manoir, in order to tell them all the particulars of the death of their dear son, which the letter of Madame de Rohan Chabot did not contain. He left them a precious souvenir of the young martyr, his carte de visite (a small photo), which, two hours before the signal for battle, Raoul had given him in exchange for his, as a mark of mutual attachment, and, in case of death, as a parting gift. M. de Montagnac and several other friends of Raoul du Manoir, who were his companions in martyrdom, also received one at the same time, which they bore to their graves, as Raoul did theirs.

Before taking leave of this heroic young man, and turning my eyes from this amiable and valiant figure, permit me to cite a short extract from a letter written to Madame du Manoir by a pious and noble lady, who was the witness and consoler of several of these glorious martyrs whose lives I relate in this book:

"Two feelings dispute my heart, happy mother! poor mother! Happy mother! for everything tells me that he whom we loved and esteemed in the camp proved worthy of himself and his past life at the moment when, in his goodness, God took him to heaven! Your son has been selected by God, madame, as a pure and acceptable offering for the peace of his Church. What a glory!"

"He was ready; God found him worthy." In these admirable words are contained the life and death of Raoul du Manoir.

"He was ready for heaven; God found him worthy of martyr-dom." I cannot close with more suitable words this account of acts of this noble-minded young martyr, and these few pages which it has been my happiness to have been able to conse-crate to his memory.

JOSEPH BLANC

I am now come to lay my humble crown on the tomb of Joseph Blanc, sergeant in the Pontifical Zouaves, who died at Castelfidardo. To one of his worthy friends, a Christian, who knew and loved him from his youth, and by whose counsel he decided to engage in the army of the Holy Father, I am indebted for the following precious details of his life and death: Noël Bernard Joseph Blanc, a law student at Grenoble, was born at Lyons, the 21st of March, 1832, of an honorable commercial family. By his mother he was descended from many noble and ancient families of Bourgogne, and what is better still, he counted saints amongst his ancestors. His infancy was signalized by a half-miraculous interference. At four years of age, although endowed with unusual intelligence, he was dumb. His venerable mother one day received a visit from a holy reli-gious, the Rev. Père Roger, who wore a large crucifix; the child, seizing it, kissed it, and said three times in a perfectly distinct voice, "Cross! Cross! Cross!" His mother, troubled and full of joy, inferred from this extraordinary event that her son would one day play an important part in the Church. His life, being too short for a glorious mission, his death realized this pres-age. The pious lady saw with delight the love of God daily developing in the soul of her only son, of which he gave each day touching proofs. Whenever he went out, although still very young, he would never pass by a church without ardently entreating to be allowed to go in and salute the Child Jesus, and if those who accompanied him refused his request, he constrained them by prayers, tears, and stamping of feet to accede thereto.

God had certainly endowed Joseph Blanc with special and great gifts. His intelligence was quick and great, his mind clear, and his memory prodigious; although but a child it sufficed for him to read his lesson to know it; later on, an entire book, in order to retain it thoroughly. To his mental gifts he joined the rarest qualities of character, an amiable simplicity, a great reserve with superiors or strangers; a good-tempered gaiety, an immense charity, an unparalleled adherence to justice and truth, and consequently to the holy Church, which is here below (if I may use the expression) the incorruptible guardian, the eternal dwelling of truth and justice. He had to struggle against evil all his life, that is against the interior evil of temptation. The gifts of his mind, the kindness of his heart, and the seductive beauty of his face multiplied the temptations round his steps, which he did not always know how to resist, and as a faithful friend who knew and loved him well said, that to be perfect he should have been less handsome; Joseph Blanc agreed, but though he committed faults at times, he deplored and detested them, and he promised his friend that if temptation sometimes surprised him he would never consent to it. His faults, however, were light, accidental, and passing, and when the terrible and bloody storm arose which threatened the Church with ruin, God found his soul pure enough to make him one of his defenders first, and soon one of his martyrs.

Before the great and supreme trial of sacrifice, Joseph Blanc had many sorrows to endure, which seemed as if God wished to prepare him by sufferings for that complete immolation of himself which He was to demand of him. He lost his good and holy mother, and all alone in the world he was near losing all his property by a lawsuit; owing to this he was obliged to go to Toulouse, where he entered and kept two terms of law at the University; then he returned to Grenoble in order to continue his studies and prepare for the bar. It was in the midst of these studies, and the preoccupation of this lawsuit, not yet concluded, that he was surprised by the Italian war, which was soon followed by the sacrilegious attempts of Piedmont. His ardent and truly Catholic soul was deeply moved, and he wrote a pamphlet entitled, *The Pope and the Congress*, in defense of the rights of the Holy See. But this was not enough for a heart which, according to the Scripture, "hungered and thirsted after justice." The departure for Rome of General de la Moricière made him understand that it did not suffice to write on behalf of the Pope when, young, valiant, and free, he could fight and die for him. What were all demonstrations compared to the shedding of blood. He left his studies, his lawsuit, the hopes of a brilliant future, and leaving the pen for the musket, he hastened to engage himself in the Pontifical Army. Arriving one of the first in Rome, he was bitterly disappointed; the generous tide which soon brought so many noble volunteers to the feet of our Holy Father had not yet set in, and for some time he was alone; the formation and organization of the Franco-Belgian battalion, which was three months later to excite the admiration and sympathy of the world, experienced those delays which mark the beginning of all great things; and it was not until after two months, when he had laid out all the money he had brought with him, that Joseph Blanc was admitted into the Pontifical Zouaves: he signed an engagement for two years, but death reduced it to three months. He was the fifth Frenchman enrolled in the army of the Holy Father.

Thanks to his great talents and soldierly bearing, he quickly regained lost time, and shortly after his engagement he was appointed sergeant. He was on the point of receiving a commission when the invasion of the Piedmontese obliged him to start for Loreto; this was to be his last halt. He was beloved by his comrades; up to the day of battle, and at Castelfidardo, he was the object of their admiration and their pride: he fought with a courage and impetuosity unequaled, and even among all these heroes he was particularly distinguished. Several of his surviving comrades have said that no one did more injury to the Piedmontese than this noble student and improvised Zouave. For a long time Joseph Blanc fought fiercely, yet unwounded; but towards the end of this desperate struggle he fell, pierced through the chest by two balls. His death was not immediate; they brought him to the Church of St. Francis of Assisi, where a religious priest administered to him the last sacraments. He lived yet a few hours; they wanted to bring him to the hospital of Asimo, but he, feeling himself to be dying, asked as a favor to be allowed to expire at the foot of the holy altar, in the presence of that God for whom he had given his life. His request was granted, and soon after Joseph Blanc drew his last breath, pronouncing the sacred names of Jesus and Mary, and also that of St. Joseph, his patron, and

For a long time Joseph Blanc fought fiercely...

the patron of a happy death. Protected by this great and powerful saint, purified from his past faults by the tears of penance and the blood of martyrdom, his soul went to receive in heaven the reward promised to those who "hunger and thirst after justice," and of whom our Lord Jesus Christ has declared "they shall be filled," and that "the kingdom of heaven shall belong to them."

FELIX DE MONTRAVEL

Felix Gabriel Fleury de Tardy de Montravel was born at Joyeuse, on the 23rd of October, 1831, of one of the noblest families of Vivarais. No matter how far back you trace the history of his ancestors, you find only examples of ardent faith and self-devotedness. One of his forefathers, Richard de Montravel, was killed at Bouvines, in 1214; another of his grandsires accompanied St. Louis to the Holy Land. Almost all the members of this noble family served their country in the army; other members, too, served France by praying for her in the cloisters. Many of them died on the battlefield, but all were faithful to their proud Christian device, *Sanguine nobilis, virtute nobilior*: "Noble by blood, nobler still by virtue." The Viscount de Montravel, father to our martyr, was worthy of his ancestors and of his son. Deeply learned, a distinguished linguist, and member of several academies, he gave all his life an example of the most perfect virtue, and when he died at Lyons, on the 19th of October, 1856, his confessor said of him, "that he died a saint, bearing to heaven his baptismal innocence." His worthy and noble wife, Mary Francis Susanna du Ronchet de Chazotte Carrièr, soon followed him to the tomb, dying also in the odor of sanctity, on the 13th of June, 1857. With such examples on earth, and such protectors in heaven, their numerous family walked without straying in the path of duty and piety, and God permitted that one of them, whose short history I am going to relate, would push the spirit of faith and sacrifice even to the heroism of martyrdom.

Felix de Montravel spent his childhood and youth at Joyeuse, where he, as well as his brothers and sisters, was educated by his virtuous and learned father, and whence he drew that deep sense of duty and honor, and that ardent love for the church and France. After the death of his father and mother, he went first to Paris to complete his studies, and then returned to Lyons, where, in order to avoid idleness, he occupied himself for some months as clerk on a railway between Mâcon and Bourg. In these different places, he was an example to his companions by his regular and pious conduct. It was at Lyons that he met M. de Cathelineau, who was leaving for Rome with the intention of organizing a body of troops, or knights of St. Peter, whose members were to furnish their own outfit and a sum of money necessary to support them for six months. The noble soul of Felix de Montravel was enamored with the beauty of such a project, and he immediately resolved to be one of the first to engage amongst these mercenaries of a new kind. He started for Rome without saying adieu to his brothers and sisters, determined on making the sacrifice of his life to the Sovereign Pontiff; he, too, from the moment of his departure, to that of his death, was haunted by the thought that he would have to shed his blood for the cause of Holy Church. The choice troops of M. de Cathelineau not succeeding, he joined the Pontifical Zouaves, and the charming qualities of his mind and heart soon gained the love and esteem of his comrades. The Viscount de Poly speaks of him with particular affection in his book entitled, "Recollections of a Pontifical Zouave." On the eve of the battle of Castelfidardo, he prepared himself like his comrades to appear before God, for whom he was about to fight, and piously kneeling in the sanctuary of Loreto, he received, with faith and love, Him who was waiting to crown him in heaven; and, on leaving the Holy Table, he told his cousin Chazotte, who was also a Zouave, the dark forebodings which filled his mind. God had decreed that before ascending Calvary, each of these pure and noble victims should share in the agony of the Garden of Olives.

Felix de Montravel was one of the first to climb the heights occupied by the Piedmontese. He was near this farm which was so heroically defended by a handful of his comrades, and had just knelt down to reload his musket, when he was struck in the left eye by a ball which went through his head. To die on his knees, with his face towards the enemy, was an attitude

...and had just knelt down to reload his musket...

worthy of a soldier and a Christian! When falling, "Long live France! Long live Ardeche!" he cried. Ardeche was his native country, the cradle of his family, the home of his brothers and sisters. It is not known if life exhaled with this last and touching remembrance, but they were his last words. His cousin, Ferdinand de Chazotte, who saw him fall, bent over him and found him bleeding and motionless; after kissing him, he had to leave to continue the battle, and from that moment nothing has been heard of Felix de Montravel. His body must have been thrown by the Piedmontese into the ditch common to all the other dead of Castelfidardo, and his family could not procure any relic of their martyr.

His noble family showed itself worthy of him, and one of his brothers, Theodore de Montravel, when he heard of his death, left home and friends to take his place in the Pontifical Zouaves, where he was received with open arms by the old comrades of his brother. He is there at present in quality of sub officer, under the command of M. de Charette, in company with his two cousins, MM. Ferdinand and Paul de Chazotte (The date at present being late 1861). Happy family, and foretold blessed, to be thus represented in the army of faith, justice, and truth! These brave young men had the happiness of visiting, eighteen months after, the immortal field of Castelfidardo, and of praying on the tomb, where lie mingled together the bones of so many heroes. They prayed for the souls of these glorious dead, or rather they invoked their aid for France and for the Holy Church of Jesus Christ. Alas! they did not find there a single headstone, not even the sacred sign of redemption; the Piedmontese, these Mussulmans of the nineteenth century could not suffer that the Divine Cross would point out the place where the mortal remains of their victims lie, fearing lest it should become the resort of pilgrims. But their tyrannical surveillance can not prevent the pilgrims to Loreto from kneeling down when passing this field consecrated by the blood of the soldiers of Pius IX; neither can it prevent the good country people of the neighborhood from sighting as they see it, and making a hasty sign of the cross, saying to one another, in a low voice, and with accents of pity and admiration, "This is the field of the martyrs!" Not far from there is another common moat, where the Piedmontese have thrown the remains of their dead, after having burned them, either through fear of pestilence or in imitation of the Pagans. There no person kneels, no person prays, and strange and mysterious, no exterior sign, no monument of mourning or triumph, points out to the passers-by the burial place of these sad conquerors. They decreed a monument, they even laid the first stone, at which ceremony two poor children of the once pious and illustrious house of Savoy were condemned to preside; but rain, wind, and storm, scattered both materials and workmen. The monument, forcibly suspended, has not been erected up to the present, and the only memorial which has until now signalized both the place and the anniversary of the battle of Castelfidardo on the part of the Piedmontese has been a scandalous and sacrilegious reunion, which begins by a vain show of prayers and ends by a garrison ball! Hideous peals of laughter, such are the funeral prayers of the conquerors of Castelfidardo. The conquered of this great day have met a better fate; eulogiums, prayers, and tears have not been wanting to them, and powerful and universal sympathy has been offered to their families. The family of Felix de Montravel was privileged in this way, and they ought to bless God in the midst of their tears for the sentiments of deep and lively regret which the death of their dear and glorious martyr has evoked from all hearts. The entirety of Vivarais shared in their affliction and their joy; the clergy of the diocese headed many touching and pious demonstrations. The Holy Father received, with particular kindness, the brother of the martyr who had come to replace him, granted him several audiences, and bestowed on his family important and numerous favors. In fine, the friends of Felix de Montravel caused to be erected in the church of Joyeuse, at the end of the chapel of Montravel, consecrated to St. Louis, King of France, a monument destined to perpetuate his heroic devotion. It is of white marble, simple and chaste, bearing the following inscription:

TO THE MEMORY

OF

FELIX GABRIEL FLEURY DE TARDY DE MONTRAVEL,

VOLUNTEER IN THE PONTIFICAL ZOUAVES,

BORN AT JOYEUSE, 23RD OCTOBER, 1831,
KILLED AT CASTELFIDARDO, 18TH SEPTEMBER, 1860,
WHILST FIGHTING IN DEFENSE OF THE CHURCH.

HIS FRIENDS IN THE VIVARAIS.

Lower down are engraved these words of Scripture: *"Stat-uerunt dimicare et confligere fortiter eo quod civitas sancta et templum periclitarentur."*

Like his companions in martyrdom, Felix de Montravel was wept for by all good Christians, and like them, he is crowned in heaven; and, in speaking of these pure and noble victims, we may apply to them the words of our Lord when speaking of Mary, the sister of Lazarus: "They have chosen the better part, which shall not be taken away from them."

CHAPTER VIII

EDMUND DE MONTAGNAC—LANFRANC DE
BECARRY—ALPHONSUS MENARD

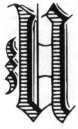P TO THIS I HAVE SPOKEN OF THE French volunteers who died on the day of Castelfidardo. I will now speak of those who survived their wounds some time, beginning with those who died first. The reader, therefore, will not be surprised that the history of those who lived longest will be more developed, as it is only natural that their martyrdom, having been of longer duration, the details thereof and edifying features, are more numerous.

EDMUND DE MONTAGNAC

Count Edmund de Montagnac was descended from a noble and ancient family of Berry. One of his ancestors, having given his life for the faith, had made his race illustrious, about six hundred years ago, when fighting under the walls of Jerusalem, to snatch from the Mahometans the tomb of our Savior. The young and worthy descendant of the Crusader was destined to die in his turn, in the flower of his age, near the sanctuary of Loreto, whilst disputing with modern Mahometans the tomb of St. Peter, the center and supreme seat of Christian truth in this world.

Edmund de Montagnac started for Rome, bearing with him the great souvenirs of his race and the blessings of his parents; and though he did not die on the battlefield of Castelfidardo, he was the first who died from the effects of his wounds. He expired the 20th of September, two days after the battle.

Here are the terms, truly worthy of a martyr and the cause for which he died, in which M. de Saint Cernin, one of his companions, describes his death, when writing to his father, the Marquis de Montagnac:

> "Summon up all your courage as a Christian and a man.
> Heaven has gained him whom you have lost; it is with
> God you must now seek your son. The same courage
> which animated our dear comrade and young hero

during the battle sustained him in the hospital. The ball
went through his left arm, and lodged a little above
the stomach. His pain was not intense, but it was long.
Struck down on the 18th of September, my poor friend
died on the 20th, at six o'clock in the evening. My name
certainly meets your eye under very sad auspices: in
order that it may not be too dark in your memory, I
will tell you, that, although older than your son, I was
his friend. I fell near him, struck by a ball in the head,
so that captivity and pain have united us more closely.
All that friendship could do, my comrades and I have
bestowed on him: he has had all the helps that religion
and art could give; but he was marked out for heaven.
My attention seemed to please him; he always asked
for me. His hand was pressed in mine the entire of the
last sad day. He often spoke to me of his friends, and
his last message was: 'Tell them that I always loved
them.' He gave me a parting kiss for you, his broken-
hearted parents and for you I kissed his brow, when
closing his eyes in death. My head is still very weak,
and I am ill-suited for this sad mission. Pardon me,
Monsieur; I have not used sufficient caution; but I have
seen such great grief, and seen such strength granted
to prayer, that I feel certain your dear son will obtain
by his prayers consolation for your broken hearts."

Noble young man! tender and courageous Christian! you are
worthy to be a martyr, and we must thank God, who seems to
have so well chosen his victims, or rather his elect, at Castelfidardo, for having left in the world some souls resembling in
faith and devotion those he has called to Himself.

When the news of the death of the young Count de Montagnac reached Berry, the clergy and inhabitants of the little town
of Cluis (this being the residence of the deceased) were deeply
grieved, and the people came in crowds from the country to
attend the funeral service, celebrated in the church of Cluis for
the soul of the hero. The enthusiasm and devotion of the worthy Curé communicated itself to his audience, and when recalling the remembrance of the Crusader who died for Jesus Christ
at the siege of Jerusalem, he cried with the eloquence of faith:

"Thanks to your courage, noble young man, you have caused
the noble scenes of an heroic age to revive. Your ancestors

Battle of Castelfidardo.

rejoice in their tombs, and bless you for causing their virtue to flourish again; and your beautiful soul, when entering Paradise, was saluted by another hero, a martyr, who died about six hundred years ago." By a singular coincidence, the church of Cluis was undergoing some repairs, and they discovered, under the cement, a black band with the arms of Gancourt quartered with that of the De Montagnacs. This black cincture extended on the walls was a privilege formerly granted to the founders or benefactors of churches on the occasion of the death of a member of the family, and which seemed to reappear on this occasion, to add additional luster to the martyr, whose funeral obsequies they were then celebrating.

LANFRANC DE BECARRY

The history of the martyrdom of young Becarry will be short, like his life. Younger still than George Miyonnet, he was not seventeen when he joined the Pontifical Army, and while yet but a child, entered courageously into the path of sacrifice. To fight against evil even to the shedding of blood, to immolate one's self willingly to justice and truth, is an energetic and manly act. This heroic act the noble child undertook without hesitation, and accomplished without weakness or regret. Lanfranc de Becarry was born at Metz, in 1844. He received from his parents an inheritance of faith and virtue. He grew up in so pure and bracing an atmosphere, that love of duty and energy of mind outran his years, and at sixteen he had the soul of a hero in the body of a youth. This manly soul manifested itself at the time of the Italian events. The Marquis of Becarry, knowing that his son would find in his paternal inheritance more of noble traditions and grand examples than of wealth, endeavored, from his birth, to form his dear child, by solidity of faith and a careful education, to be a man and a Christian. On hearing of the formation of a Pontifical Army, under the direction of General de la Moricière, he proposed to Lanfranc to join it. In case of success, he saw for him on one side a military future, and in case of reverse, he hoped that the mind of the noble young man would be elevated by sacrifice, and that he would return to him grown greater for his devotedness. When he made known to Lanfranc his idea, the poor child did not at first understand the greatness of his mission nor the extent of his sacrifice. But, as soon as he arrived at Rome, his noble mind understood it at once, and his devotion to the cause of the Holy See, his energetic resignation to all sorts of sufferings, rendered doubly painful by his extreme youth and the presentiment of his approaching death, soon raised this child of sixteen to the level of all those martyrs and heroes whose lot he shared. Exercise, fatigue, and severe discipline, he bore all with a calm energy, strength of mind supplying what was wanting in strength of body. The first time he met R. P. Stumpf (the Providence of the Pontifical Zouaves at Rome) he was returning from a long military march, and seemed exhausted.

"Well, my good child," said the kind father, "you are very fatigued!" pointing to his equipment. "This is very heavy."

"Oh, no! father," replied the noble boy, "I am stronger than you think!"

When saying this he was teeming perspiration the while, and his feet were covered with blisters. "But, my child, if you get maimed, or perhaps killed, what do you think will your parents say to that?"

"Then, father, it will be a great consolation to them to know that I died for God whilst defending the Sovereign Pontiff."

During the long, last march from Loreto to Castelfidardo, like his comrades, he patiently endured all the fatigue. "Bah!" they would say to one another smiling, when their feet bled, and they felt themselves ready to fall under the burden; "it is for God and the Pope we are suffering!" and pursue their way courageously At Castelfidardo young Becarry fought bravely, and fell in the thick of the fight, pierced by three balls. Taken first to the church of Castelfidardo, he was next day brutally placed on a horse and thus dragged to Asimo, without any person propping him in that long journey of nearly twelve kilometers, with his poor leg, which was shattered by three balls, dangling. Stripped by the Piedmontese on the battlefield, suffering great pain, constantly hurt by his cowardly conquerors, the young martyr of sixteen bore his cross on that long and painful way with heroic courage. At first his wounds did not seem mortal, and they hoped to save his life. He was convinced, too, that he would recover, and he wrote to his father on the 30th September, saying, that on his return to France he would join a regiment in order to enter at St. Cyr after two years' service. He asked some money to enable him to go to Rome after his recovery, to receive the blessing of the Holy Father, and to ask him for a cross or a medal, as he considered he had well earned one. Nevertheless, when he arrived at Asimo, he made a general confession, which he repeated a few days after. On the 5th of October, owing to a hemorrhage, which greatly aggravated his case, he wrote a few lines without signature to his parents, which terminated as follows:

"Come, my poor mother, come with my father; you alone can cure me." Alas! they could not do it now; bad care finished the work of the Piedmontese bullets; their child was past recovery. One of his comrades, who was also in the hospital, on his return to France, related the revolting conduct of the Italian infirmarian who had care of him. This wretched man, having remarked that young De Becarry had hidden his purse under his pillow, was incessantly hovering round his bed, and would bend over him by way of caressing him, hoping, at the same time, to steal his little treasure unperceived. The poor child ended by conceiving such a horror of this man, that it was in terror he saw him come near his bed. This infirmarian had also charge of giving him broth and Bordeaux wine three times a day to repair, if possible, his exhausted strength; he only gave it to him once, reserving the surplus for himself, and when he drew his last breath, this man took the bottle which was near and slowly swallowed the contents. "Delicious!" he said, smacking his lips, and passed gaily on to another. In spite of all this ill-treatment and suffering, Lanfranc de Becarry died calmly and holily. Like the greater number of the martyrs he was deprived of the consolation of seeing at his death-bed his father and mother, who hastened from Lorraine to embrace him once more, but did not arrive at Asimo until twelve hours after his death, when they heard with grief that their child was no more; they had, however, the consolation of hearing that he died as became a hero and a saint. The morning of the battle he had been condemned to walk twenty steps behind the others as a punishment for not having been able to wake in time after the forced marches of the day before. His commanding officer came to see him on his bed of suffering, and not thinking him in danger, asked him, smiling:

"Well, Becarry, are your arms all right?"

"Yes, my commander; I have washed them in my blood."

"But how, poor child, did you manage to get three balls?"

"I understood," replied the dear child, "that you had ordered me to walk twenty steps *before* the battalion, and I obeyed." The Marquis of Pissy, who lavished his attention on all those wounded at Castelfidardo with truly paternal affection, was particularly touched by the strength of mind of young De Becarry. He often went to see him, and said a last adieu to him a few moments before his death, when the dying child said to him: "I am like Job extended on a dunghill;" and, as a matter of fact, his wound was frightful to look at; but the calm and happy face of the martyr was still more admirable to behold.

He confessed, received Holy Communion with great love, and died on the 17th of October, at a quarter past eleven at night. Up to his last sigh, it was he who consoled his friends and companions, and if he saw them weeping, he repeated to them with the greatest tenderness: "I have made the sacrifice of my life to God, and He has accepted it. Weep no more!" Thus died, at the age of sixteen, this amiable youth, pure and holy as a child, brave and energetic as a man: thus it was that the so-called mercenaries of the Pontifical Army knew how to offer and consummate the sacrifice of their life for the cause of the Sovereign Pontiff, their Father, and of their Mother, the Holy Catholic and Apostolical and Roman Church.

ALPHONSUS MENARD

Young Alphonsus Menard was nineteen years of age when he died at the hospital of Asimo, on the 23rd of September, from the effects of his wounds, five days after the battle of Castelfidardo. The account of his sacrifice is contained in letters which I shall quote, one from his father, the other from a friend announcing to this courageous Christian the death of his son. These letters are short, and contain few particulars; nevertheless, the reader will agree with me that they contain sufficient to make known the glory of the martyr. Here are the two precious documents; the first is that of Monsieur Menard:

"Yes, my commander: I have washed them in my blood."

"BORDEAX,
15th October, 1860.

"SIR,

"The hope which the discovery of my son's name on the list of the wounded at Castelfidardo gave me, has been of short duration. Nothing remains to me now but the grief of having lost him, and of not being able to find out soon enough the place of his sufferings, which have been so long, and during which he was deprived of the care and consolation of his parents. It is not, as you see by the papers, a father and brother he leaves to mourn his loss, but a mother, sister, and two brothers. On remembering the holy cause for which he suffered so much, after having generously fought at the age of nineteen, I am greatly consoled, since I am convinced that he for whom we weep is now in possession of the martyr's crown. Will you please show to your readers the letter announcing to me the death of my child. The hearts of others, who have been afflicted like ourselves, will find a comfort in reading this letter of my religious friend, whose name, I regret, I have not been permitted to give; but I do not wish to deprive the public of the benefit of his sentiments, from which I have derived so much consolation.

"Respectfully yours,
"ARMAND LOUIS MENARD."

"POITIERS,
8th October, 1860.

"DEAR MONSIEUR MENARD,

"When I saw by the papers that your child was mortally wounded, I could not contain my grief. My God! what an affliction. But I remembered, at the same time, your courage and faith, and therefore I hoped that God, for whose cause your son shed his blood, would help you to endure this terrible blow. Perhaps, as yet, you know nothing certain regarding the fate of your dear crusader; but do not be deceived! Poor father! receive with courage; but I am mistaken. Man of faith and courage, read with pride the communication which I have just received, and which is, as it were, the acceptance on the part of God of the sacrifice you have made to Him and the Church! I have the painful duty of announcing to you the death of young Alphonsus Menard, which took place at Asimo, on the 23rd of September, whither he had been brought after the battle of Castelfidardo. I request of you to inform the family of this glorious martyr, that he died as became a Christian hero: this is the only consolation worthy of these admirable families, who have given their children for the defense of right and justice. Thus, dear Monsieur Menard, are perpetuated in your family its noble and rare traditions, and which you have so well known how to transmit to your child. No doubt your heart bleeds, and this sensibility is quite lawful; but, with the great apostle, you will say through your tears: "I suffer, yet I am not confounded!" It is very consoling to think, that owing to their baptism in blood and the plenary indulgence granted to them by the Holy Father, our courageous crusaders have already entered into the possession of that imperishable glory which is the lot of those who have fought the good fight. It is consoling, too, to think that all this noble blood has not been shed in vain: they have been conquered, say the people of the world, and that is all; little they know that those who triumph with us are our martyrs. Do they not know that the redemption of the world has been acquired by the most Precious Blood, and that it is by the shedding of the best blood that society will be regenerated? I hope, dear sir, that you will find in these thoughts some alleviation of your bitter grief; for, no matter how bitter your grief may be, we are still Christians, and therefore unlike to those who have no hope. I weep with you, I hope with the same confidence and faith, and I affectionately press: your hand."

CHAPTER IX
ROGATIEN PICOU

ROGATIEN PICOU, OF AMIABLE AND holy memory, belonged to one of those respectable families of merchants, with whom simplicity of manner, nobleness of mind, and staunch faith, are hereditary. He was born at Nantes, and losing his mother when only two years of age, he was brought up by his vigilant and pious father, and under the care of an elder brother, who was his godfather, and to whom he was deeply attached. His rare talent and anxiety for instruction induced his father to impose great sacrifices on himself in order to educate him. At nine years of age he entered the seminary of Guerande. He made his first Communion at twelve, and imbibed in the participation of the Body and Blood of Jesus Christ those sentiments of faith and devotion to the Church, which made him a true Christian in life and a martyr in death. He went from the seminary of Guerande to that of Nantes, where he distinguished himself by his talent and good conduct. Ignorant of the difficulties of life, as children generally are at fifteen years of age, he never dreamt of the severe, onerous sacrifices which his father had made for his sake. One day that he was studying with less industry than usual, his brother made known to him their family circumstances. The soul of this generous child was thunderstruck at this revelation. "Since matters are thus," he cried, with tears in his eyes, "I will finish my year at the seminary, but I will not return. It was wrong of you, brother, not to have made known to me before the trouble of my father. I have two arms as well as you, and I will work like you to help him." And the noble child did as he said. He gave up, not without a broken heart, his dear companions and studies, and on leaving the seminary, he obtained a situation in a library. There, at least, he had books, and could employ his leisure hours usefully. "I am only happy in the midst of my old books," he said smiling, "with this difference, that science

Rogatien Picou.

now passes through my hands and not through my head, as formerly." Forced to pass through his hands, science did pass through his head also, and aided by his books, he completed, in a few years, his literary education.

The reading of the great authors, and of the great Catholic orators, charmed him, and from their works he drew those sentiments of knightly devotion which led him soon after to death and immortality. The four years which he spent thus were the happiest of his life. He divided his free time between prayer, study, and the home circle. A few amiable and pious companions shared his friendship. This simple life filled him with such happiness, that he was sometimes frightened at the dark shadows which crossed his mind. "Oh! brother," said he to his dear Alexis, "how happy I am with you; yet I dare not dwell long on my happiness, as I feel some strange forebodings coming over me. I am afraid of my happiness: something tells me it will be violently dashed from me!" Alas! the violence which was to dash from his lips the cup of happiness was the revolutionary storm which was gathering thick and fast on the horizon, the distant rumblings of which were heard with terror throughout Europe, presaging everywhere blood, tears, and ruin! Rogatien heard, as well as all Catholics, the prophetic warnings of the bishops and the Sovereign Pontiff, and the cry of alarm from the Holy Church which was outrageously attacked; but he also heard, with a heart thrilling with enthusiasm and love, the grand news of the formation of an army of Catholics to defend the Pope against his miserable aggressors. It was then that his noble heart showed itself, as we shall see by the following words, which alone would serve to immortalize him:

"To God and his Vicar, I have neither fortune, talents, birth, nor influence, to offer; but I have my blood, and I give it to Him!" God accepted the free oblation of the generous child. "Can I," he writes, "make a better my strength than to consecrate it, according to a beautiful expression, to the defense of a saint under the leadership of a hero? I long for the title of Soldier of the Cross." A few days before his departure for Italy, he wrote to his brother: "It will cost me a great deal to part from my poor father. My heart is broken at the very thought. But, if we meet again, the Church will be avenged and saved, and will reappear more brilliant than ever, and then glory and benediction to the families who have furnished defenders for so holy a cause! God will watch over his children, and He will hear my prayer that you may be spared to my father." He started full of faith and zeal for the holy cause to which he had devoted himself, bearing with him the benedictions of his father.

He was not the first son that this poor father had seen set out on a distant and perilous expedition. Five years before, weeping, he had embraced another of his children, who went to fight in the Crimea under the glorious banner of France, and that young soldier nobly fell in a strange land. The departure of Rogatien, therefore, opened a still bleeding wound, but the generous father knew how to restrain his grief in order not to discourage his son, and the sacrifice which the citizen had made for his country, the Catholic renewed, without hesitation, for the cause of Him, whom a young Breton styled, with sublime simplicity, "the Father of all Countries."

On his arrival at Rome, Rogatien Picou joined the corps of M. de Cathelineau, and after that the Franco-Belgians, where he cheerfully endured all the hardships of military life. From this to the 18th of September his life was that of a volunteer. On the battlefield of Castelfidardo he fought courageously, and fell at his post, struck by a ball across the right thigh. After the battle the Piedmontese, according to their custom, stripped him of all he possessed, taking even his uniform; then they rolled him, bleeding, in a coarse sheet, and placed him on a wagon, which carried him slowly to Asimo, suffering cruel pain at each jolt. At the improvised hospital at Asimo his bed was a confessional; beside him lay young Lanascol, before him Count de Chalus and Joseph Guerin, who were not better lodged than he, all four of whom were destined to die and receive, almost together, the martyr's palm. From there he wrote a letter to his family full of faith and resignation to the designs of God, and full of hope, too, for he did not think his wound was mortal. This letter, which was delayed by the Piedmontese, for I do not know what reason did not reach his poor father until after he had heard of his death. It was one of his comrades in the hospital who announced, in the following terms, the sudden and unexpected end of Rogatien:

"I have sad news to tell you. My brave comrade, Picou, was very well at five o'clock in the evening, on the 27th of September, and said to me, "*Au reroir,*" because I was leaving the hospital of Asimo to go to the Jésu. Just as I was starting, he called me, and said: 'Carré, call the doctor, a blood vessel has burst in my wound.' I ran to the end of the hall to call the doctor, and returned as quickly as I could. He said, 'Help me; I am dying.' I did help him, but in a few minutes I had no longer a comrade. He died at Asimo, on the 27th of September, at seven o'clock in the evening. I am very lonely since, and his death has greatly upset me.

"HENRY CARRÉ."

Thus died this pious and amiable young man, who had offered his life's blood to God and the Church. He had not, like the greater number of his companions, the consolation of receiving the last sacraments; but martyrs baptized in their blood require no other purification, and he could say, when expiring, the prayer of the French missioner of Tonquin, when being led to suffer: "I desire to receive absolution, but that is impossible. O my God, accept, then, my contrition for confession, and my blood for Extreme Unction. I do not feel my conscience burdened with any grave sins, yet I am not purified. But Mary will obtain for me contrition, and the sword will be my anointing."*

Rogatien Picou died the same day, and almost the same time, as Arthur Chalus; they dug but one grave for these two generous defenders of the Holy See, and their coffins lie side by side. The Church, following the example of her Divine Spouse, makes no exception of persons, and shed over their mortal remains the same blessings and prayers, and she will forever associate, in her gratitude and her praises, the name of Rogatien Picou with that of Chalus, Pimodan, and her other illustrious martyrs.

---

* The last letter of M. the Abbé Cornay, martyred in Cochin-China on the 20th September, 1847.

CHAPTER X

PAUL DE PARCEVAUX—HYACINTH DE LANASCOL

HE PONTIFICAL ARMY COUNTED THREE German cousins Paul de Parcevaux, Hyacinth de Lanascol, and M. de Goësbriant. The two first died from the effects of their wounds, the third received a ball in the forehead, and, according to the quaint expression of his cousin Parcevaux, he owed his life to the solidity of his Breton head. Thrice happy family, which had the glory of giving a confessor and two martyrs to the cause of Holy Church.

PAUL DE PARCEVAUX

Paul Mary Thomas de Parcevaux was born, in 1831, at the castle of Tronjoly, near St. Pol de Leon, and the first years of his life flowed calmly by in the midst of his brothers and sisters, and under the watchful eye and fostering care of his mother. He drank in the faith with his mother's milk, and the love of God and the Church were sacred heirlooms in his family, and increased in his soul according as he grew in years. From his childhood he evinced great vivacity of spirits, a large heart, and quite a joyous turn of character. His gaiety brought sunshine wherever he went, even on the battlefield and in the hospital at Asimo. During the course of his studies, which he commenced at the college of St. Pol, continued at Brugelettes, and terminated at Redon, he was beloved by masters and scholars. His frank, genial nature made friends of all who knew him. Nevertheless, when studying the law at Paris, in order to pass an examination, he knew how to limit his friendship to a few worthy companions, whose principles were conformable to his own. On his return to Bretagne, he lived almost entirely in the country with his widowed mother, and by his gaiety became the true joy of the family. Always a tender and respectful son, affectionate and devoted brother, a man of the world, and at the same time a perfect Christian, he was the same everywhere, amiable and beloved. He was very witty; therefore, his conversation was naturally lively and quaint; but he was never known to wound charity in all his jokes, a virtue which is so often absent from worldly meetings.

A letter from one of his old college companions, whom he met at Paris, announcing his departure for Rome, determined him to set out also and offer his heart and arm to the Holy Father. It was not until the eve of his departure that he announced his project to his mother, and asked her consent and blessing. The pious mother gave both weeping, but without hesitation, and Paul de Parcevaux bade adieu to the dear land where he was born, which he was never again to see, and where he left the best part of his heart. He embarked for Italy with five other volunteers, and these brave young men formed the nucleus of that little troop of French chasseurs, which increased rapidly, and became, after some time, the Franco-Belgian Battalion. Paul de Parcevaux made part of the expedition to the Grottoes (an early battle in the Crusade of 1860 and the first of the Franco-Belgian Battalion) which, under the command of M. de Pimodan, routed the troops of Zambianchi. He distinguished himself in this unimportant but glorious affair, and attracted the eyes of his chiefs by the joyous energy of his character. This energy never flagged for one instant during the three months' hardship attendant on the organization of the Franco-Belgian corps, and he bore all the trials with a soldierly cheerfulness, which diminished them considerably. He was, however, beginning to despair of ever measuring his strength with the Garibaldians, and he was already asking himself if his military life was to be limited to the expedition of the Grottoes, when the news of the Piedmontese invasion in the Marches and Umbria came to reassure him on this point. He was about to engage now with Garibaldians of the worst kind, Garibaldians disguised as Bersaglieri. He had just been appointed sub-lieutenant, when his division received orders to rejoin, by a forced march, the bulk of the Pontifical Army at Loretto. His gaiety sustained him and his comrades during this painful journey, and even on the battlefield. But he knew in these circumstances, as he had always done, how to give to serious and divine things the best part of his time and heart, and he prepared himself to fight and die like a Christian. One

131

of his companions declares to have seen him, a little before the battle, confessing, kneeling in the ditch.

When the battle commenced, Pimodan's column rushed to assault the position of the enemy; The Pontifical skirmishers drove back the Piedmontese; and the farm and house of Cascines fell into the hands of the Pontifical Zouaves. But the Bersaglieri, crowning again the summit of the hill, and sheltered behind the underwood and thick hedges, sent a shower of balls on the heroic battalion. "Forward! To bayonets!" was the cry of the chiefs. Paul de Parcevaux repeated it to his company, rushing on himself first; but scarcely had he gone a few steps when he fell, struck by a ball in the breast. "I am dead," said he to his comrades, who pressed around him; "I am killed; but no matter!" They took him into the farm-house, and one of his comrades, named Thiriet, gave him a crucifix to kiss. This act of pious charity touched his heart, and later on, one of his principal injunctions to his family was to write to this brave young man to thank him. However, Paul de Parcevaux was bleeding copiously, and whilst his friends were undressing him to staunch the wound and facilitate his breathing, the combat continued around him. The house took fire, and his comrades, after having surrendered, were obliged to get out through a window. His clothes were all burned, and nothing remained to him but his shirt. They took him with the other wounded to the church of the neighboring village, then to the ambulance of Castelfidardo, and finally to the hospital of Asimo, which he only left for heaven. It was from Asimo he wrote to his mother, the day after the battle, telling her of his wound:

"MY DEAR MOTHER,

"On the 18th, General Pimodan tried, at the head of about four or five thousand men, to force the position of the Piedmontese, numbering from thirty to forty thousand, who were strongly entrenched about a mile from Loretto. We could not conquer them; but the resistance of the volunteers stupefied the Piedmontese. In three-quarters of an hour the army retreated, and the artillery had abandoned their cannon, whilst we still held the position we occupied at the beginning of the action. Wounded, I admired the tenacity

"Forward! To bayonets!"

of my fifty companions, who only surrendered at the order of Goës briant, when the house took fire, and only three were without wounds. They let me down by a window, and myself and comrades were brought away by the Piedmontese. At the roll-call of my company that evening at Loreto I think not more than five or six answered. The Bretons have paid their tribute nobly. De Conëssin, De la Vïenville, and De Rennes are prisoners, though, I think, not wounded. Le Camus, De Guingamp have nothing. Lanascol has three balls in the same leg; but I hope they will be extracted without amputation. My neighbor at the left, a sergeant in my division, has four balls, but not a serious wound. He is a very respectable boy, named Jolys, from the neighborhood of Rennes, and was very attentive to me, especially the first days, when I could not raise myself without assistance. Quéré Plouvern has a ball in the thigh, but, I believe, not dangerous. De Chalus has two balls in the legs, and my friend Cavailhès two wounds of a bayonet in the breast; but he will probably get over them. As to Goësbriant, he replaced me when I fell, and in three minutes after he was struck by a ball in the forehead; but, thanks to his Breton head, he will escape with a magnificent scar. As to myself, I was struck with a ball in the breast, which came out in my right side. My wound is severe; but I feel better to-day, and I think I shall be able to pull through. When going to the battle I asked God to make me do my duty well. As to my wound, I am not more afraid of death now than I was on the 18th. In Bretagne I would have a small chance of gaining heaven so easily. If I die here I hope to die well. If people hear cries of pain in the hospital they also hear peals of laughter. They are taking away my pen and ink. Good-bye; and I hope to see you again! If God sees fit to take me to Himself, my last thought will be of you.

"PAUL DE PARCEVAUX."

These heroic sentiments never left him for an instant until his death; and if he was a brave and high-spirited soldier on the battlefield, he was still more admirable on his bed of suffering. His resignation to death, his lively faith, ardent piety, and confidence in God filled with astonishment and admiration all who saw him. When his sufferings gave him a moment's respite, his old gaiety returned, and they could say that, faithful to the end to his amiable nature, he was affable and smiling, even in pain and death. Thus he even made friends on his hospital couch, and two or three of the inhabitants of Asimo, who came to visit the poor prisoners, were specially attached to him, and gave him touching proofs of their affection and sympathy. One of them was a young priest attached to that bishopric, who cared for him like a brother, spending hours by his bedside, and during the twenty-four hours before his death he never left him, except to say Mass for the intention of his dying friend. Paul de Parcevaux had one great comfort before dying: he could press in his arms one of his brothers, who hastened from Bretagne in order to nurse him, or at least to bring him the embraces and last benedictions of his mother. The hero received his brother with great delight, and for several days they enjoyed each other's society; but although his state did not seem alarming, he persisted in saying that he should not be cured, that he could not be cured, and that he did not wish to be cured; and that if it was sweet to live to see his mother, he thanked God for the favor granted him of dying for the cause of his Church. "No!" said he, "I do not wish to live; the conditions in which I find myself for appearing before God are so satisfactory, that I fear if I were cured I should not be so well-disposed again." His last wishes were contained in these words: "My soul to God, my body to Our Lady of Loreto, and my heart to my mother." It is really the will of a martyr. The days preceding his death, his confidence in God and ardent piety seemed to increase: "My God," he would say, "have pity on a poor sinner; have mercy on my soul! Immaculate Virgin, do not abandon me! St. Joseph, assist me!" From his bed of suffering he was the consoler of those suffering near him. Seeing one of his comrades weeping over him, he said, with a feigned bluntness: "People do not cry here! Let them cry in Bretagne. I am nothing to pity." To another of his neighbors, whose wounds forced him to cry with pain, he said, with sublime energy: "Be silent! Is it a Breton I see crying? Such a sight would only delight those Italians around us!" He was alluding to the doctors, surgeons, and infirmarians, who cared them, God knows what way! He received, at his own request, the Sacrament of Extreme Unction on the eve of his death; and, although everyone thought he would die then, he said, with prophetic assurance: "Do not think I am dying now; I shall not die until two in the afternoon tomorrow."

Nine days before, he said to the Abbé de la Treiche, who attended him to the end: "I will not die for ten days." And so it was about two o'clock he died next day, Sunday, 14 of October, twenty-six days after the battle. On Saturday morning he commissioned his brother to bear his adieux to all his friends and companions, who, like him, were nailed to a bed of suffering. The tears which they all shed, on receiving this sad message, proved how much his good heart had gained their affection. Divine goodness seemed to surround his last moments with the sweetest consolations, and a celestial serenity shone on his forehead, giving to his dying features an inexpressible charm. His dying eyes brightened, when he saw or heard anyone praying for him. "His resignation to death," writes the young Italian priest, of whom I have already spoken, "or rather his joy at giving his life for God, was so great that it shone on his features. One would fancy that he already had a foretaste of the happiness he was going to enjoy in heaven! I still contemplate him smiling sweetly at all who approached him." He died calmly, like a child sleeping in its mother's arms, and he was already dead before his brother perceived it. His last wishes were executed to the letter. He had left his soul to God, and it would be impiety to doubt that God had received the soul of the martyr into the glory of paradise. He had left his body to Our Lady of Loreto, and there it rests against the altar in the underground chapel. He is buried at the Gospel side; and at the other side are the remains of the Spanish General, Lopez, who died for the Holy See while defending Ancona in 1797. In fine, he had left his heart to his mother, and on the 27th of October, M. Louis de Parcevaux arrived at the Castle of Tronjoly from Loreto, and presented to the noble and courageous lady the now inanimate heart of the martyr. Unspeakable moments, full of heart-rendings and consolation, when the cries of grief forced by nature, and words of thanksgiving inspired by faith, leave the lips and heart of the Christian mother. Three days after the martyr's heart was borne in procession from the Castle of Tronjoly to the parish church, where it lies awaiting the Resurrection. More than seventy priests and five thousand persons accompanied this procession. We cannot picture ourselves a more touching spectacle than that of this heart, encased in a modest urn, chastely ornamented, and borne by the companions of the martyred hero. On this urn was laid a white crown and the Cross of the Order of Pius IX, which the Holy Father had sent him a few days before his death. The urn was carried by M. de Kermel of Quimper, and the strings were held by M. de Goësbriant, cousin of the deceased, and M. Jolys of Rennes, his devoted friend. All these noble youths wore their uniform as Pontifical Zouaves. Along the way those of the country people who could not possibly attend came out to piously salute the funeral cortege. Kneeling, with joined hands and eyes wet with tears, they seemed rather to be invoking a saint than praying for a deceased person. And they were not wrong: it was a saint, a martyr of the Holy Church, whose heart was passing before; and, cold though it was in death, it seemed to enkindle around it faith, devotion, and love. By special permission of the Bishop of Quimper, a monument was erected in the Church of Cleder, the parish of Paul de Parcevaux, over this precious part of his mortal remains. This monument will remain as a great lesson for generations yet unborn, and fathers will show it to their children, while relating to them the heroic history of the martyr, to whom they can apply the beautiful words of the Book of Maccabees: "He who died has left not only to young men, but to the entire nation, the souvenir of his death as an example of virtue and courage."

HYACINTH DE LANASCOL

Hyacinth de Lanascol was some years younger than his cousin Paul de Parcevaux, and died a few days after him. Like him, he received from his parents a thoroughly Christian education, at the College of St. Francis Xavier, at Vannes, and waiting only for God's own time to bring forth worthy fruits of salvation. Without being quite as pious, perhaps, as his mother wished, he never gave up the practice of frequenting the sacraments;

Hyacinth de Lanascol.

and notwithstanding the allurements of youth, and the dangers which surrounded him in Paris, far away from his family, lively faith and a deep sense of duty always held sway over his heart. The Italian events, and the appeal made to Catholics by General de la Moricière, brought out clearly the generous sentiments of faith and devotion which filled his heart. On the 3rd of April, uninfluenced by example, and of his own proper notion, Hyacinth de Lanascol wrote to his father, asking his permission to leave for Rome. He was then at Paris, on the eve of standing an examination. His good father, seeing no urgency in the present situation, and anxious to try the resolution of the young man, answered by desiring him to wait for the examinations, and that he would decide afterwards regarding his other request. Hyacinth obeyed, but when he saw the Roman affairs hastening his friends, companions, and even cousins, to start for the Army of General de la Moricière, he could endure it no longer, and wrote a pressing letter to his mother, from which we give a few extracts:

"MY GOOD MOTHER,

"You have given me an education which you alone could give me; taught me principles which I will ever retain and never deny. I regret being so far away from you, for perhaps soon I shall have to leave you for a long time. You know that I have already expressed a wish to join the Papal army; and though I have not spoken of it since, I have not changed my opinion; I merely delayed my departure as my father wished. But, dear mother, I know your religious sentiments, and you remember when we were reading the papers together we were indignant at what was passing. Here, I assure you, I cannot see what is happening without deep horror; and if the Pope is in danger, I, who am convinced of the truths of religion, and am devoted to it, ought to fly to his aid. I heard that Oliver de Kermel and Gaston du Plessis have already set out. We will fight in a good cause, and we are not afraid of dying for our faith. I wish also to join this crusade, for the more Frenchmen there are the better. I would wish to enlist all my friends, and it will not be my fault if I do not bring several of them. Dear

139

mother, there are already in the Papal army a host of my companions. I must join them. God will help us, for it is a holy cause; and though I have often offended Him, He will pardon me. Yes, dear father and mother, in the age in which we live they would fain do away with religion, assassinate its visible head, erase the name of God from the minds of men. Well, it is for us to resist these wretches who would overturn the Church if they could; it is for us to defend our principles; and he who says he is convinced of the truth of this, yet recoils before the sacrifice necessary to maintain and defend it, does not know his duty. The hour approaches: before leaving I would wish to spend some time with you in the dear Cheffontaines (the Château where Lanascol grew up), where I was born, and where I spent my childhood. Would that I could see you once again! Amice is in heaven praying for me. Dear parents, give me your blessing. We will communicate together—"

This letter was written on the 20th of June. M. de Lanascol thought the moment had come to fulfill a great duty, and anxious that his son should leave under the care of M. de Cathelineau, he wrote to have him return home immediately. Hyacinth reached the castle of his father on the 27th of June, at eleven o'clock at night. He longed once again to see this well-beloved country, which he was, perhaps, leaving forever. What grief was mingled with the caresses of his parents! What sadness was mingled with the joy of seeing those whom he was so soon to leave! The day after his arrival, at five o'clock in the morning, he went with his eldest sister to bid adieu to the venerable priest who had baptized him; to pray in the little church where he had received the precious gift of faith, where he had accomplished the first duties of a Christian; and to kneel on the grave of his sister and eldest brother, beside whom he rests today. Then he bade adieu to his dear Cheffontaines, and the same day, at nine o'clock, he heard Mass at Quimper, and there received Holy Communion with his father, mother, and sister; that evening he started with his father for Nantes, the first stage of this grand journey, which was to end in the hospital of Asimo, or rather in heaven, and left his native country covered with the tears, kisses, and blessings of his mother. Before leaving Quimper he wished to write to his grandfather, to bid him adieu. I will give the entire of this noble and touching letter; besides, it was an ancient and pious custom of the first Christians to preserve with respect the writings and words of their martyrs:

"QUIMPER,
"28th June, 1860.

"MY VERY DEAR GRANDFATHER,

"This is a great day for me, a turning-point in my life. I leave all those I love, perhaps never to see them again. Oh! my kind and very dear grandfather, I have not words to tell you my grief. It must be a grand cause, for in the midst of my grief I feel a ray of happiness. My poor mother is wholly resigned, and although she grieves at my departure, she is happy to see me leaving for so noble a cause. Papa, mamma, Mary, and myself received Holy Communion this morning; I did not forget you and aunt. I cannot go to see you, but mother will tell you the reasons which prevent my going to Brest: I assure you they are weighty or they could not hurry my departure like this. I must now conclude, as my time is limited. I will write to you soon again. I wish you a happy feast and good health. This is perhaps the last time I can do so, therefore I do not wish to let the opportunity pass. In a word, dear grandfather, it is a great sacrifice, and my heart is broken, and I know not when I shall see you again. But no matter, our last meeting-place will be heaven, and I am going to take the road thereto under the banner of the Blessed Virgin, which is our standard.

"Your respectful and devoted grandson,
"HYACINTH DE LANASCOL, Crusader."

We see that the noble young man, in order to assuage a little his poor heart, torn by grief of separation, had to remind himself that he was a Crusader, a soldier of the Cross of Jesus Christ. This struggle between nature and faith continued until he embarked at Marseilles: while on French soil, each tree, each wayside house, reminded him of what he had left behind.

On the eve of leaving Marseilles, the 2nd of July, he wrote to his father: "I have passed through a beautiful country when coming here, but all the fine scenery and mountains remind me of my dear Bretagne and the dear Cheffontaines, where I spent my childhood. Thither fly all my thoughts and affections. When I think of you and my happy home my only consolation is the beauty of that cause which I am going to defend. My body is far from you, but my heart is with you and my country. This morning we rose at six o'clock in order to make a pilgrimage to Our Lady of La Garde: we heard Mass there, during which we all burned a taper. We also bought some medals. Everyone has decided on defending religion to the last extremity, and is quite gay; but it is a calm gaiety, breathing happiness, and springing from a tranquil conscience. We are all Bretons, and we fraternize like old acquaintances."

We see the letter ends more cheerfully than it commenced. The society of new friends, the sight of the Mediterranean, which was to bear him to the scene of action, and above all the protection of Our Lady of La Garde, brought peace and calm to his youthful soul. From this to the day of the battle his natural vivacity never left him, and the enthusiasm of youth and faith sustained him in all his trials. The stay at Rome, which often does more harm than good to weak minds, only developed his faith and piety, as we shall see by his letters. When starting for Terni he wrote thus to his mother: "I think we shall soon have a battle; but we are calm, and trust in the cause we defend. I will fight under the protection of the Holy Father, and that is the best! I would not wish to die on the battlefield in any other sentiments." It was in these sentiments he did die, but not on the battlefield, as he was destined to languish more than a month in the hospital at Asimo before going to enjoy in heaven the martyr's crown. Before describing his suffering and death I will relate the part he took in the battle of Castelfidardo, and which he describes himself in a letter which he wrote to his father from his hospital bed. I shall reproduce the greater part of this interesting letter, the history of one of these valiant volunteers, novices in the military career, and soldiers more through devotion than vocation:

"War is a horrible spectacle! You should be there with
the motives which guided us, to understand it. In the
morning we had to cross a small river which separated
us from the Piedmontese, the only bridge of which
they had barricaded in order to prevent our crossing. The firing commenced before we reached the
other side, but it was not much. We advanced then
to the plain in skirmishing order, and in a short time
we had taken the first bulwark, on the top of which
was a house: this was a farm-house, surrounded by
straw. The Piedmontese were entrenched on a thickly-
wooded height behind it. We rested for about two or
three minutes behind this farm, then in a moment we
passed out at both sides to charge the enemy. There
was great disorder just then, bullets whizzing around
by thousands; the air was actually burning. Well, dear
father, thanks to the Blessed Virgin, whose medal and
scapular I wore, as also to the cross, and St. Anne,
whom I did not forget to invoke, I passed through
this grape-shot for the first time in my life with the
coolness of an old soldier. harging and firing without ceasing, I was squatted with two or three others
behind a large tree, where we could see the Piedmontese. We were firing some time when a ball, fired from
behind, went through the back of a man named Ker-
moal, who was near me, and came out by the arm.
This first wound did not discourage him. As for me
I felt a certain painful impression at the sight of my
friend's blood, which was flowing in waves beside me.
I made a few steps forward, and found myself alone
in the midst of this shower of balls. I vowed to all
the saints in heaven, and I thought of you. I fired
at a Piedmontese whom I was looking at for some
time, but I cannot say if it was him or his companion
I struck. Just as I had fired, a spent ball grazed my
thigh; fortunately it did not enter, as, between ourselves, I have my two legs today. That was all very well
so far, and I reloaded my musket with my companions.
We were all in the open country, not a tree to shelter
us. Whilst I was loading, one of ours, a Breton named
Alfred du Bandiez fell, struck by a ball in the region
of the heart, and at the same time I was struck in the

left calf. I discharged my musket, and as I could still walk, I advanced to reload it again. I had not gone far when I was struck by a second ball in the same leg, which slackened my pace a little, but did not stop me; but again, just as I leveled my gun, a third ball struck me in the same leg (it seems the Piedmontese were determined on having this leg), and I fell like a clod of earth: others, too, fell around me. The battle lasted about two hours longer, and I cannot describe to you all I suffered during that time: I was bleeding copiously. All I know is that during these two hours I heard only three things: the whizzing of bullets, the cries of the wounded, and the cries of the combatants. When the battle was over the Piedmontese rushed like tigers to pillage us. With no regard to our wounds, they ill-used us in a dreadful manner. I had six hundred francs, which they took without leaving me a sou. They also took the medal given me by the Pope, and my pistols. Such is, dear papa, the story of my encounter." In the same letter the noble young man adds, with tearful emotion: "This is a great misfortune for the Church; it occupies me unceasingly. What will become of the Church? What will become of society if the Revolution triumphs? As to us, we have done our duty; God will protect us and reward us, at least in the other world."

The wish of the young crusader was not long in being granted, for this letter is dated the 30th of September, and he died on the 20th of October. Divine Providence granted him one great favor before his death. His mother, hearing of his situation from M. de Goësbriant, had already started for Italy, and on the 8th of October, Hyacinth, seeing her enter the hospital, thought it was an apparition from heaven. What joy filled the heart of mother and son! how sweet were the tears they shed! it is what all good mothers and affectionate sons can picture to themselves. This joy during the first days was unmingled with sadness, for neither Hyacinth nor his mother thought there was danger ahead, and looked on his cure as a work of time. The first word of Hyacinth, as soon as his joy permitted him to speak, was:

"Oh! I did expect you! I knew that either papa or you would come." And from that to his death, twelve days after, he lavished the most tender and delicate marks of affection on his mother. During the twelve days passed by the bedside of her son in the hospital, surrounded by all those wounded heroes, the greater number of whom were to die, Madame de Lanascol never heard a complaint or murmur 'midst the moans which their pains forced from them, and she was greatly edified at their admirable sentiments of resignation and piety. "One feels," she writes, "that God's blessing is with them." She saw her nephew, Paul de Parcevaux, die. "My good and dear nephew, Paul de Parcevaux," said she, "preferred to die, and his death has been that of a saint, as has been that of young Guerin. My dear son, placed between these two holy souls, was not so fortunate as to be cured and return to his family; but when the moment of sacrifice came he made it with courage and resignation, without expressing the least murmur or regret."

Thursday, the 18th of October, three days before his death, his case taking a grave turn, they thought it better to administer Extreme Unction. It was his mother who proposed it; he was not the least disturbed, but said, calmly: "Do the doctors think I am dying?" He received the last sacraments with angelic piety, and when the ceremony was over he called Sister Louisa, who attended him, and said to her: "Sister, I am going to heaven; when I am no more do take care of my mother." A moment after, was alone with his mother, his head leaning on her shoulder, he raised his eyes to hers, and said: "Mother, if I die, you will not leave me here? You will bring me with you, to be buried beside my sister?" This was his sole dying request. The poor mother answered by tears and kisses. Twelve hours before his death they resolved on trying the amputation of the left leg, which they hoped up to this to avoid; but it was too late. Hyacinth himself earnestly begged it, and after again receiving Holy Communion, he courageously gave himself up to the surgeons; but as they could not administer chloroform they did not wish to try it, as, owing to his weak state, he would probably sink under the operation. Therefore he had

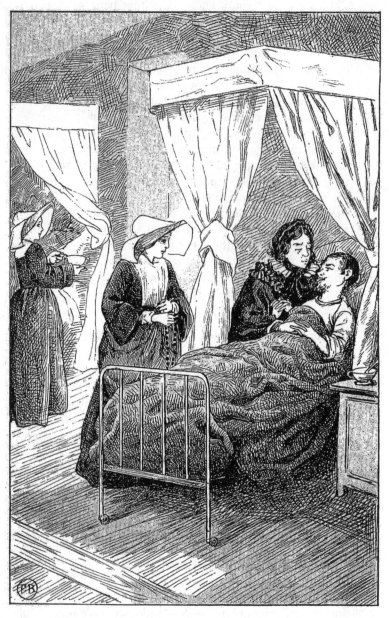

"Mother, if I die, you will not leave me here? ..."

to await death, which he did with serenity and resignation. It is impossible to say which was the more admirable, the resignation of the son or the heroic constancy of the mother, the more edifying during the long agony of her dear child. "My God," the dying child said, "your will is mine! Your will is mine! Your will is mine! Do with me what you will, and as you will!" He laid a stress on these words, which showed his complete abandonment into the hands of God. He added soon after, "My God, I love you! I wish to love only you! I love only you!" One time that his mind wandered, he said, "I have been killed," "for God," added his uncle, M. le Count du Russel, captain of a vessel, who was kneeling at the foot of the bed.

"Yes, for God and for the glory and defense of the Church," added his mother.

The witnesses of this sublime scene were making vain efforts to restrain their tears, when the courageous mother said: "Do not weep." Seeing her dear child agitated, she asked him if he wished to have prayers recited aloud?

"Yes," said he. The priest read the prayers of the Church, and then stopped. "Pray again," said the dying hero."It comforts me." He loved to hear them praying, and as soon as they commenced he remained quiet. Suddenly he raised himself up in his bed, and said, with angelic calmness: "I am dying; I feel it."

"My child," said his mother, "we will recite the Te Deum; you know your father often says it." Then he fell into his agony, which was that of a child. His mother embraced him without even giving a sigh. Thus, in the midst of the hymn of thanksgiving, the soul of the martyr calmly winged its flight to heaven, on the night of the 20th or 21st of October, at one o'clock. O incredulous poor people! Poor enemies of the Church! Poor insulters of the Papacy! tell me, have you ever seen any of yours die thus? Tell me, if in your sad annals you have ever met with a scene as imposing and sublime as this.

How shall I tell of the honor paid to the mortal remains of the martyr when his mother brought them back to his native country, of the immense throng which filled the Cathedral of Quimper, the prayers, tears, and praises poured forth over his tomb, and of the great crowd which accompanied the remains of the heroic volunteer to their last resting-place? I will only

mention one incident which took place at the moment of separation before the half-opened tomb. Just as the prayers of
the Church were ending, the priest, whose voice was firm and
almost triumphant, suddenly betrayed a little emotion, and fal-
tered. His eyes were fixed on a lady in mourning, who advanced
from the center of the crowd, approached the tomb, and kneeling down, was absorbed in grief and prayer; this lady was the
mother of the martyr, who, heroic to the end, had come to bid
a last adieu to the mortal remains of her beloved son.

CHAPTER XI
ARTHUR DE CHALUS—JOSEPH GUERIN

E MUST NOT SEPARATE WHAT GOD has united. I will not, therefore, separate in my narrative Arthur de Chalus and Joseph Guerin, whom God united in sacrifice and death: two pious and amiable young men, two pure victims, two strong and meek souls, who overflowed into one another during the agony of agonies, and who almost fled together to heaven, like the first martyrs who fell in the arena whilst giving each other the kiss of peace. Both were Bretons, and, probably without knowing it, they met more than once at the foot of the altar, in the church of Nantes, adoring the same God, whom they received on their chaste lips and into their loving hearts, and mingled their tears over the misfortunes of the Church and its august Head. Their positions in life were very different; and certainly they would have been astonished if, a few months before their departure for Rome, and enrollment in the Pontifical Army, they had been told that they were destined to handle the musket, wear the same uniform, and to fight and die side by side.

Count Arthur de Chalus belonged to an ancient and noble family of Lower Maine. He was born at Nantes, where his father died in 1845. Losing his mother when only five years of age, he spent the winters in his native country with a pious old aunt, who loved him tenderly; during the remainder of the year he lived at the Castle of Doré, the residence of a brother-in-law whom he loved, and of his sister, whose children grew up with him, and always looked on him as an elder brother. This solitary life, occupied solely by the love of God and his family, had a special charm for our young and thoughtful Christian, whose soul, already strong, fortified itself still more by prayer and study. Faith and charity were depicted on his brow, and he showed by his example that in truly Christian lives these two sisters are never separated. The parish of Doré always saw him

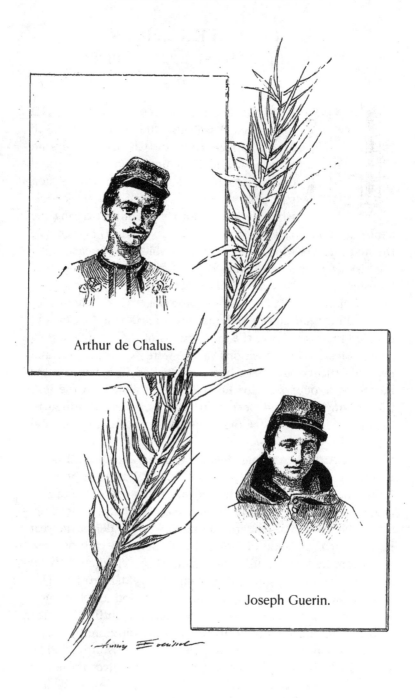

Arthur de Chalus.

Joseph Guerin.

at its head every time that any public devotions were going on, and each year when the *Quarant' Ore* (40 Hour Devotion) came round, he was always the first and last at the foot of the altar where the Eternal Victim reposed. The Rosary was his favorite devotion, and the year before his death, he erected, at his own expense, a beautiful cross of granite in the parish, which will tell for many years the faith and piety of the martyr. He loved the poor as the suffering members of Jesus Christ, and bestowed on them a large part of the wealth he inherited from his father. His charity went even beyond ordinary misery, as we shall see by the following trait, which shows that he knew how to give delicately as well as generously. One of his old companions of Brugelette, having involved himself by a rash act, wrote to him after some years saying how bitterly he regretted his foolish step, but that he must remain in the service now, as his father absolutely refused to buy him out. (During this time in the French military, it was possible for yourself or someone else to buy out your service obligation). Shortly after, Arthur de Chalus was traveling in Algiers, where this young man was stationed. "Well," said he, on meeting him, "the noble trade of arms has no charms for you?"

"Alas, no!" replied the unwilling volunteer.

"How much would be required to buy you out?"

"Fourteen hundred francs."

"Here are two thousand; you can repay me when convenient." Such was the life of Arthur de Chalus.

That of Joseph Guerin was very different. Born of honest and comfortable trades-people, he lived in another retreat, in the bosom of another family. He entered the great seminary of Nantes with the intention of becoming a priest. When the Italian revolution and the departure for Rome of General de la Moricière showed the necessity and possibility of the formation of an army of Catholics, the two young men, animated by the same feelings, actuated by the same motives, left their families and homes. The resolution of Arthur de Chalus resembled that of many others, and the life which he abandoned was the same as that of the greater number of the French volunteers of Castlefidardo. Only that his merit was perhaps greater, as his predominant fault, in embracing the rude life of a Zouave, was a love of good living and independence. "But," as he said himself, when answering the objections of his friends, "only for that I should have no merit." It was not so with Joseph Guerin, who was, I believe, except his friend M. Pinsonneau, the only volunteer of the Franco-Belgians who left the soutane for the uniform of the Papal Zouaves. It was neither through caprice nor inconstancy he deviated from the ordinary routine, but through a special vocation, which he explains himself in a letter, as we shall see later on, and which God justified in a striking manner, by giving to this noble young man the martyr's crown. For the rest, Arthur de Chalus and Joseph Guerin knew very well what they were going to do in Italy: they went to die there, and their sacrifice was premeditated and already consummated in their hearts, before they had left France. Some time before his departure, Arthur de Chalus made a pilgrimage to St. Joseph of the Oak, and when returning from this celebrated sanctuary, he said to his sister, who accompanied him:

"What have you asked for me, through the intercession of good St. Joseph?"

"I have asked," she replied, smiling, "for an amiable and pious wife."

"And I," replied the young man, seriously, "asked for the grace of a holy and happy death." His mind was so noble, and naturally disposed to sacrifice, that he did not understand the surprise or congratulations of his friends, and his only answer to them was: "My action is a simple one; therefore, I do not understand your astonishment." One of the humblest but most devoted friends of Arthur de Chalus admired his sacrifice and imitated it. This friend (I use the term designedly) was the gardener of the castle. Thoroughly devoted to his young master, this worthy boy asked and obtained the favor of accompanying him, and, like him, he joined the Pontifical Zouaves. Someone advising him to return to Bretagne, where he would be happier than in Italy, he replied: "M. le Count was happier than I, and he has gone." This good servant added:

"I have only my person, and I willingly give it. My one desire is to see the Holy Father, and receive Holy Communion from his hands, get his blessing, and then die for him; I hope then to reach heaven." Nothing is more touching than this simplicity! Arthur de Chalus left Nantes with Joseph Guerin, and they reached Rome together. At Marseilles they met George D'Heliand, traveled by the same steam-boat, and became great friends. Afterwards they had an audience with the Sovereign Pontiff, who blessed them with special affection, and kneeling side by side, they received from his hands the Body and Blood of Jesus Christ. The sight of the holy Pope Pius IX., his touching kindness and sublime resignation made a deep impression on Arthur de Chalus. "Oh!" wrote he to his aunt, "if all those who speak against the Pope had the happiness of seeing and hearing him, in spite of their wickedness they would soon change their language."

After the rude labors of military apprenticeship, after the fatigue of the forced march to join General de la Moricière at Loreto, came the day of the first and last struggle, for which Arthur de Chalus prepared himself like all his comrades. At Castlefidardo he fought like them, and fell in the midst of action, struck by a ball in the thigh. They transported him with the others to the hospital of Asimo. He was calm and intrepid on his bed of pain: he had fought as a soldier, he was suffering as a martyr. There he met again Joseph Guerin, his compatriot, his friend, and his brother-in-arms; both were already marked with the seal of the elect; they mutually consoled and helped one another until their last breath. Once installed in the hospital, Arthur de Chalus wished to acquaint his family of his situation, and wrote to his aunt the following letter, full of simplicity and strength of mind, and in which we find reflected the last gleam of his amiable gaiety:

"ASIMO,
23rd September, 1860.

"MY DEAR AUNT,

"You have, no doubt, heard ere this the result of the battle that we fought on the 18th of September, near the town of Loreto. After having bravely fought, and taken a house in which the enemy was lurking, I received a shot which broke my right thigh, leaving two balls in the flesh. They tell me that I shall return, but that it will be a long time. However, if I am lame, we can play backgammon oftener together. Excuse my scribbling, and excuse the brevity of this letter; embrace all those I love, and, be assured, my dear aunt, of the affection of your nephew,

"ARTHUR DE CHALUS."

Alas! the good young man was deceived, or rather he deceived his poor aunt regarding his real state. He was never more to play backgammon with her: already the angels held suspended over his head the martyr's crown. A few days after this first letter, feeling his end approach, and no longer able to hold a pen, he asked his dear Guerin, who was in the next bed, to write a letter, which he dictated, and which was to be the last.

"ASIMO,
29*th September.*

"MY DEAR AUNT,

"Last night, having suffered a great deal from a hemorrhage, I could not sleep, and am very weak. The excellent Guerin, who is lying near me, had the kindness to offer to write to you. I do not know what God has destined for me. Shall I ever have again, my very dear aunt, the happiness of seeing you, my sister, and all who are dear to me? May the holy will of God be done. In leaving France, I made the sacrifice of my life; I renew it with happiness, notwithstanding the pain I feel of dying far from my country and friends. Embrace for me my sister, brother-in-law, nephew, and nieces. A thousand remembrances to all our relatives, friends of the town and country, and please accept, my dear aunt, the respectful affection with which I subscribe myself,

"Your nephew,
"THE COUNT DE CHALUS."

After having thus attested once more that he accepted death joyfully, and sent this last testimony of love to those he was leaving behind, Arthur de Chalus gave his thoughts and affections to that Divine Master to whom he had offered his life. He uttered no words but those of faith and resignation.

Joseph Guerin, who received his last sigh, testified that he died like a saint, often repeating: "I am content to die!" After his death he was robbed of all he possessed; not even his rosary beads could be found to send to his family. They buried him at Asimo; and the Piedmontese would not allow an inscription recalling his courage and sacrifice to be engraved on his tomb. But the tomb was marked, and the day will come when the free and grateful hand of the Church will trace there the glorious sign of martyrs.

Joseph Guerin survived his friend some time; but before relating his death I must go back to where I stopped, that is, where I left him starting for Rome. Like Arthur de Chalus, he made his sacrifice, and knew that he was facing an almost certain death. One of his friends reproaching him with the folly of his project, he replied, with vivacity: "Well, yes; I am wrong, it is true; but I err with the martyrs who went and offered themselves to the executioners. You are right, if you like, but I prefer being in the wrong with them. Blood is necessary to appease the anger of God; I give mine."

He relates the interview which took place with his parents, when he made known to them his resolution. I do not know of anything more beautiful: it is faith and heroism in all their purity:

"I entered my mother's room, my rosary beads in my hand. 'You promised me a bead, and you have never given it to me; but I prefer waiting until you are a priest, as you can then procure me one blessed by the Holy Father.'

'No, mother; I promise to give you one very soon.'

'Yes; but I would also like to have some relics.'

'You will have them, too.'

'How will you get them?'

'That is a secret.'

'Are you going on the foreign mission?' (She knew a missioner who had a great many relics.)

'No; it is a bead blessed by the Pope I will send you.' A sudden thought struck her:

'Are you going to join La Moricière's army?'

'And why not? How often have you not said to me that you would like to be a sister of charity, in order to attend the

155

wounded soldiers of the Holy Father?' My mother remained silent for a moment; tears started to her eyes:

'Have you reflected, prayed, consulted?'

'Yes, mother; I have told all to my director. Yesterday I communicated at the altar of the Holy Rosary, recommending to God my journey.'

'Ah! why did you not tell me, as I would have gone to Holy Communion, too?' Again she asked me: 'Have you reflected, prayed?'

'Yes, mother.'

'Well, go, my son, if God calls you.' Here she could no longer restrain her tears. My cousin Jules came in then, and left immediately to call my father, who, when he came, asked what was the matter with my mother. I said it was nothing; that she could not resist a too great sensibility; but that if he wished to know all, to come away and I would tell him. I brought him to my own room, and related to him the conversation I had just had with my mother. He threw himself into my arms, weeping, and said:

'I will not be less brave than your mother; I have already lost a son; but if God asks me for another I will give him. Do you intend giving up the Church?'

'Yes, for some months, as a soutane is unsuited for the battlefield; however, if God does not take me to Himself, I expect to receive sub deaconship on my return.'

"My father accompanied me in a few visits which I had to make previous to my departure. My mother was busy making preparations for my journey. The evening I went to bid adieu to the venerable Curé of Epine, my father also came. As soon as they met, they threw themselves into each other's arms and burst into tears. I cannot describe my feelings, but casting my eyes on a crucifix, I thought of Pius IX. My cheerfulness returned, and I consoled them. The next day I went to visit the tomb of St. Philibert for the last time, and recommended myself to his protection. My parents accompanied me to the carriage, and when embracing them I looked up to heaven and said to them:

'If we do not embrace again on earth, we will meet above. Adieu in heaven!...

"When I was alone, I thanked God for having given my parents so much fortitude. 'They are worthy of having a martyr for a son,' said I to our Lord; 'grant that it may be so, if it be your holy will.' From time to time I cast a glance towards Noirmoutier, the church, the castle of St. Philibert, my father's house. Nevertheless, I was calm, as I knew I was going where God called me. When crossing the canal, I intoned the canticle of Our Lady of Victory, asking her to protect me in Rome, in the camp as well as on the battlefield; then, like a child, I laid before her my resolutions regarding my military life, and ended by the canticle of St. Emilian:

"'For one's country 'tis well to arm one's self, But for God and his holy laws 'tis nobler far to die.'"

Another pupil of the seminary, M. Pinsonneau, who started from Nantes with him, relates a few incidents of their voyage from Nantes to Marseilles. From the beginning the soul of Joseph Guerin manifested the same faith, serenity, and energy which it did later on on the battlefield and in the hospital of Asimo. "Just as the last whistle of the train sounded, I felt what it was to leave, perhaps forever, without having said a last fond adieu to my mother. I wept like a child. My dear companion consoled me and exhorted me to have courage. 'We are starting,' said he; 'let us recite the *Te Deum* in thanksgiving for the favor God has bestowed on us by calling us to die in his cause, and the *Veni Creator* to ask the light of his Holy Spirit, and to obtain a safe passage.' We recited several other prayers, especially the *Magnificat* and our Rosary. We tried to sleep: Guerin slept soundly all night, but I could not. We spent Saturday visiting several churches in Paris. At Our Lady of Victories we asked God to bless the defenders of His vicar. On returning to our hotel, the thought of my mother made me weep bitterly, but I had near me one who soon raised my drooping courage. 'Rome,' said he; 'we must only think of Rome.' He was always the same, gay and cheerful. Ah! how grateful I am to God for having given me such a companion: the sight of him was quite enough. On Sunday we heard Mass and communicated at the church of the Jesuit Fathers, and left Paris the same day at two o'clock. On our way we were sometimes prey to an emotion which I cannot describe, thinking of those we left behind. Guerin was the first to shake it off, and opening his 'Imitation of Christ,' his eyes fell on the forty-seventh chapter of the third book, which begins with these words:

'Son, be not dismayed with the labors thou hast undertaken for Me; neither let the tribulations which befall thee quite cast thee down.' He showed it to me, smiling, and continuing to read, he again pointed to me the passage:

'Thou shalt not labor here long, nor shalt thou be always oppressed with sorrows.' The entire chapter alluded to what was to happen to him later on. Thus, for instance, this passage: Thou shalt not then say: *Who shall deliver me from the body of this death?* for death shall be no more, but never-failing health.'"

During the remainder of the journey, as they could not be always conversing, he appeared absorbed in meditation, which he left only to read a chapter of the "Imitation," or to recite his office. On his arrival at Rome, he was incorporated in the Franco-Belgian battalion, and the young seminarist was not long in wearing with perfect ease the uniform of the Papal Zouaves, and handled his musket as if he had been accustomed to it all his life. To an angelic piety he joined a French gaiety and bearing, which won him the love of all, chiefs and comrades. The stay at Rome, the audience of the Holy Father, the sight of the relics of the martyrs, the admirable monuments of the life and passion of our Savior, such as the crib, the holy stairs, the table at which the Holy Eucharist was instituted, and all those treasures which make Rome, as it were, an immense and living reliquary, delighted him and filled his soul with an ardent desire for sacrifice. We can judge of the truly celestial sentiments which filled his mind, on reading a letter addressed to one of his old superiors of the seminary at Nantes, and which will live in the annals of the Church as an eternal monument of faith and charity:

"DEAR AND VENERATED FATHER,

"What must you think of me? Are you surprised at my resolution? Yes, dear father, I am now a soldier, a soldier of the Sovereign Pontiff. My only regret in leaving was that I could not get Monseigneur's and your blessing. My conscience had long since spoken. I knew that in an age like the present, in the midst of this frightful overthrow of principle, in presence of the unparalleled crimes committed or premeditated against the Church and all that is sacred here below, in presence especially of the complete and strange security of well-meaning and even religious minds, there will never be, there cannot be, too many examples or protestations of devotion to the Holy See, truth, justice, and honor. After such reflections, I resolved to start, and I have done so. You will say that I have only acted as a Christian. To obtain the blessing of God, I received Holy Communion that morning, and at seven in the evening I was on my way to Paris. During the journey I recited the *Veni Creator,* the office of the Blessed Virgin, and the Rosary, in company with an excellent comrade whom Providence sent me, and then I slept contented. And why should I not? Was not my good angel watching over me? At Paris I communicated again at the altar of the Archconfraternity. Could I go on my passage without asking my mother's blessing? After several incidents, more or less remarkable, we arrived at Rome on Wednesday, the 8th of August. It would be impossible to describe to you the impression which the sight of the Eternal City produced in me. I was in the center of Christian souvenirs, of Catholic traditions, and I felt beside myself. It was no longer Rome that I saw, its monuments or wonders, but the footsteps of apostles, martyrs, and saints of all ages, the illustrious pontiffs, the thousand souvenirs of piety and faith.

"One relic, above all others, attracted my attention: this was the Holy Table where our Savior instituted the Blessed Eucharist. I could not take my eyes off of it. How many lessons did it not contain, alas! only too appropriate to the evil misfortunes of the present time. 'My God,' I said, 'what a proof of thy love; I vow fidelity to Thee; love for love, sacrifice for sacrifice.' This table, formerly covered with gifts, pious offerings of munificent kings and princes, is today empty! What hands, even in the worst days of our history, could consummate such a sacrilege? French hands. Is there no law on earth responsible to Divine Justice? What

Frenchmen have dared to commit, Frenchmen must repair. And if it be pleasing to God, I willingly give my blood instead of gold. I have had the happiness of seeing the Holy Father four times. Yesterday he admitted to a private audience the old volunteers of M. Cathelineau; I was of the number. We were in the Vatican gardens; he came with touching simplicity and stood in our midst (picture to yourself a father surrounded by his children), and spoke familiarly to us:

'My children, the Papacy is in danger, in greater danger than anyone thinks, but, with young men like you defending it, we can not fail to triumph. I have been obliged to break up your corps; but you will remain with your Pope, will you not?'

With one voice we all replied, 'Until death!'

'Very well, very well, I congratulate you,' he continued, 'heaven will grant you special blessings; I am happy to have you near me.' These words of the Sovereign Pontiff, the melancholy sweetness of his look, the charming and paternal simplicity of his manners, the ineffable mingling of sadness and resignation, grief and confidence, united to the irresistible majesty of misfortune portrayed in his features, held us spellbound, and we were breathless. At length, with one voice and heart, we cried, loudly:

'Long live Pius IX! Long live our Father! Long live our Pontiff King!' Oh, dear father, had you been only there!

"Again I offered to God, in presence of his Vicar, the sacrifice of my life for the great and holy cause of the Church. I heard afterwards that all my comrades did the same. I felt ready to face a thousand deaths if necessary. The sad events which we daily witness give new strength to our love for the See of Peter. It would be difficult for you, dear father, to understand the intrigues and plots of the revolutionists in the city of Rome. It seems to be the meeting-place of all secret agents from all parts of the world, whose efforts appear at this moment to be directed against the Papacy: they flatter the Romans, whom they despise, asking concessions and reforms in their name. Ah! if in a country which I know they took the liberty of saying or doing the tenth part of what they are permitted here with impunity, they would soon, thanks to the police, be conducted to the frontier. At Rome, as well as Nantes, I am faithful to my religious duties. I confess weekly, and Communicate much oftener than I am worthy, several times a week. I came here through a motive of sacrifice; therefore, it would, I think, be strange to neglect the only means which would merit for me such a favor. The step I have taken I did not take lightly, but after mature deliberation. I was not ignorant of the rocks and dangers which beset my new path; I prepared for them as well as I could, and now, with the help of God and my Blessed Mother, I hope to avoid them. Pray for me: you always took an interest in me, and am I not still your child?

"J. L. GUERIN."

I do not know, I may be wrong, but it seems to me that the drift of this letter is heavenly, and the love of sacrifice which it breathes reminds one of the incomparable epistle of St. Ignatius, Bishop of Antioch, martyr, to the Romans. There is, to my mind, in this family of saints and martyrs of all nations and ages, in the identity of their words, acts, life, and death, an irresistible demonstration of the divinity of the Catholic faith. To the end of this letter, dated 2nd of September, Joseph Guerin adds: "We expect to measure ourselves very soon with his Majesty GARIBALDI." The honest young man deceived, and it was with another Majesty, worse than he, they were to deal.

Just then Victor Emmanuel, the Catholic King of Catholic Piedmont, the descendant of an illustrious race of crowned saints, had assembled his numerous troops on the Roman frontiers, under the pretext of protecting them, and was meditating the infamous robbery of the Papal States and the massacre of the Pontifical Army. Indignation brings me back, in spite of myself, to a period which I have alluded to before. It was only by an unprecedentedly rapid and bold march that General de la Moricière, surprised by this vile ambush, could reunite the few thousand men who fell at Castelfidardo. Under these circumstances Joseph Guerin astonished his comrades by his strength of mind and energy. "He had," said one of them, "an extraordinary gaiety; his courage was more than admirable. He bore all the heavy fatigues of the march, during which we wanted for everything except faith, with a strength and perseverance which everyone admired."

"Why are you afraid?" he often said to his comrades; "if your conscience is not in peace, there is the chaplain. Our cause is the better; we fight for God; therefore, we are men of eternity; what signify the few days that we will sacrifice? I have made the sacrifice of my life to the Church and Pius IX. I am not afraid to die, and yet I am an only son and a spoiled child. Poor father! Poor mother!" This courage and perseverance were to be put to a rude trial. He fell at Castelfidardo, struck by a ball in his breast, after having fought like a lion, and for some time they believed him dead. M. de Perrodil, formerly a lieutenant in the French army, and corporal in the Pontifical Army, found him on the battlefield, apparently lifeless.

"There he was, lying on his back. I bent down to touch him; he was cold and stiff. I then knelt to impress on his pure brow a kiss of regret and love in the name of his parents. I took his scarf, and bade him a last farewell, believing him dead. He had been very brave, poor child, and had fallen a few steps from the enemy." M. de Perrodil was mistaken, as the martyrdom of Joseph Guerin was not yet consummated. They carried him first to the ambulance of Castelfidardo. As soon as he recovered consciousness, he said, in Latin, to a young Italian who was near him:

"If you wish to write to France, write to my Curé as follows: Tell him that I die joyfully and calmly for the cause of religion and the Pope; let him console my parents with the hope of meeting me one day in heaven; earth is worth very little when compared with it. Ask them to pray for me, and thus console themselves. I love them much, very much, and my only regret in dying is that I cannot press them to my heart." The next day he was brought to the hospital of Asimo, where he found Arthur de Chalus, his brother-in-arms, whom he lovingly cared, whose eyes he closed, and whom he followed to heaven.

His martyrdom lasted seven weeks, during which he suffered intensely. Instead of murmurings and complaints, it was words of thanksgiving and joy that escaped him. "This long time," he writes from his bed of pain to a friend, "I have made to God and to the Holy Church the sacrifice of my life. Envy my

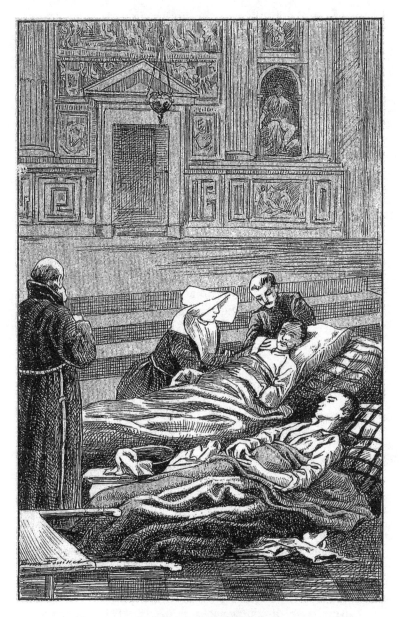

The next day he was brought to the hospital of
Asimo, where he found Arthur de Chalus...

happiness, and console my poor mother. Long live Pius IX, our Pontiff King!" "How happy I am," he often repeated, "to suffer and die slowly for Jesus Christ and His Church!" This generous athlete of Jesus Christ sipped his painful martyrdom as worldlings sip their pleasures. He knew the price of sufferings fructified by faith. He said to God, in the depth of his heart, in imitation of SS. Peter and John: "Lord, gold or silver I have not; but you have given me a treasure of suffering, and I give it to you for the salvation of your Church."

Here is what a pious lady, the foundress of several religious houses in France and at Loreto, who saw him a few hours before his death, writes: "Young Guerin, this little angel of the earth, was dying. It is very sad to see such rare souls leaving us; but heaven rejoices. The Sister told me that he wrote the evening before to his parents, which accounts for his not having given me any message for them. He was quite pale; his lips, already blue, showed that mortification had now very little to do to terminate the poor child's life, which he had so completely sacrificed to God.

'What day is this, madame?' he asked.

'Sunday.'

'Ah! I am so happy.'

'Why?' I asked.

'Because I am suffering, suffering so much.'

'And you are satisfied to suffer today?'

'Yes.' "

Here is his last letter to his parents, of which we have just spoken; one cannot read it without being moved to tears:

"MY VERY DEAR PARENTS,

"I cannot leave you forever without telling you all the love and sadness I feel; but it is God's will; let us bless and adore it. We will meet again in heaven; let this thought excite and encourage you to remain always fervent Christians. On my knees I beg of you not to give way to discouragement or despair. The sacrifice is great, but your courage is greater. Courage, my well-beloved, best, and most excellent of parents, courage! I beg of you, with tears, not to despair. God wills to have me with Him. It is hard to leave you without giving you a parting kiss, or receiving your blessing; but let us unite this sacrifice to all those which He has asked of us for the last few months. I have received no news from you, notwithstanding all my letters. I cannot believe you are angry with me; if I thought so it would make me very sad. I declare I never had the remotest intention of causing you pain; and when leaving you, with a broken heart, I told you my reasons for it. Oh! believe me, it was no falsehood. If I have offended you anyway, I most humbly ask you to forgive me, and rest assured that only sentiments of love and tenderness in your regard fill my heart. Good parents, I love you. I feel fatigued; but the pleasure of writing to you makes it light. In a former letter, I told you my wound was improving, and so it was; but unfortunately it is in my breast, and since then I have vomited a great deal of blood, which has quite exhausted me. My God, Thy will be done! Once again, then, have courage and resignation; place all your hope in God. Adieu, dear parents, dear father, dear mother, dear Jules, I must leave you, as I feel too exhausted to continue. Pray for me! I embrace you! I love you! We will meet above. Courage! Do not grieve! Your, child who loves you with all his heart,

"J. L. GUERIN, CL. M."

He died on the night of the 30th of October. His end was worthy of his life.

"On the morning of his death," writes an eye witness, "we had no idea the end was so near, and the poor child thanked me for the few little marks of attention I was so happy to render him, apologizing for the trouble he gave me. At two o'clock, p.m, swooning commenced. When I arrived, he pressed my hand, and said, in an almost inaudible voice,

'Monsieur, God is taking me to Himself! Will it be soon over? Pray for me; I will pay you back when I go to heaven. My God, I suffer greatly! but Thy will be done.... Monsieur, if you only knew how happy I am to be able to offer my little sufferings to the good Jesus, who has suffered so much for me! Do you think I shall live long?' Seeing my eyes filled with tears, and that I could scarcely master my feelings, he said: 'You must not weep or be sad, for I am very happy. Tell me, at what hour do you think I shall die?'

I said, I thought about five o'clock. 'Oh! so much the better, as I wish to receive Extreme Unction while I am conscious, in order to answer the prayers myself.' His desire was immediately granted, and he received the last sacraments from the hands of the venerable Abbé of Trèche, the French chaplain at Loreto, who multiplied himself in order to aid, physically and morally, our wounded ones, to whom he was a true father. At half-past four, feeling himself getting weaker, he asked if he had any pulse, and on my replying in the affirmative, he asked to have the *Te Deum* recited; during which a few involuntary cries escaped him, owing to the intensity of his pains. At the end of the *Te Deum* he fell into a stupor, and they thought him dead; but about half-past five he again recovered consciousness. 'O my God!' he cried, 'forgive me. I had had a thought of pride, and you punish me by prolonging my life.' Then his pains became more and more intense, but his resignation was greater still. He confided to me a secret, and told me that he wished to be buried with his parents. He continued in this state until seven o'clock. His neighbor, M. de la Salmonière, being put to bed, said to him: '*Au revoir*, we will meet again in paradise.' He grew weaker and weaker. The doctor having given him a draught to allay his pains, he got tired of it, and asked for a little wine; then, recollecting himself, he said: 'Oh, no! I will offer this little mortification to God. I have no pulse; is it not so? See, I am getting cold. Oh, thank God! Oh, may I suffer! Accept it, my God!' He was then silent; his eyes, fixed on heaven, were insensible to the light of the wax taper; he was smiling, and apparently in an ecstasy; this state lasted about twenty minutes. When he came to himself, he asked what o'clock it was:

'Half-past eight o'clock, they answered.'

'Another half hour of suffering,' he said. 'I feel a cold sweat on my forehead. What happiness! My God, I beg of you to forgive those who have wounded me. My God, accept my sufferings! Do not weep or fret, my kind friends; I am going to God. Is it near nine o'clock?' A few minutes after, that is to say, about two minutes past nine, all was over; he had given his beautiful soul to God, with a smile on his lips and peace in his heart."

It was in these admirable sentiments that Joseph Guerin, the last amongst so many precious victims, breathed his last, and who was judged worthy by God to suffer a longer and more painful agony, because a brighter crown was reserved for him in heaven by the giver of all good gifts. In that bright home he met again his dear comrades who had died before him. There he met his dear brother-in-arms, his companion in the hospital and in sacrifice, Arthur de Chalus, from whom I did not wish to separate him in this humble narrative, very unworthy of one and the other. A few months after his death, the body of Joseph Guerin was brought back to France, and the city of Nantes gave him a splendid funeral. Since then, the Catholics of Bretagne have never ceased visiting his tomb, which has become a place of pilgrimage. God has been pleased to reward the faith of these pious pilgrims, and manifest by admirable deeds the glory of his martyr. A great number of conversions and miraculous cures have been wrought there: the most remarkable of which have been officially established beyond doubt by the written testimony of doctors, and by ecclesiastical authority; all of which leads us to hope, that at no distant day, the Holy, Roman, Apostolical, and Catholic Church will solemnly place in the catalog of saints the last and most perfect of the martyrs of Castelfidardo. I would consider my labors well repaid by the worthy crowning of these pure and most heroic victims.

CHAPTER XII
THE MOTHERS OF THE MARTYRS

HE IMPERISHABLE NAME OF JOSEPH Guerin, whose sacrifice I have just related, closes the list of the French martyrs of Castelfidardo. I ought then to stop here; yet it seems to me that this work would be incomplete if I did not devote a special chapter to the mothers of these heroic soldiers of the Church; to those admirable women who by their devotion before and after the sacrifice have participated in the martyrdom of their children.

Already during the course of my recital, I have alluded to some traits of these noble characters; now I wish to complete this beautiful sketch by a closer and more comprehensive study, which will bring out in all its light the heroism of these noble Christian women, and will be, as it were, the crowning glory of our well-beloved martyrs.

Since the most holy Virgin Mary has, by a profound design of Providence, which all the doctors of the Church have recognized, participated in the Redemption as Eve did in the Fall, since this Mother of the Savior has become the new and true mother of men, whom she brought forth on Calvary, as she did the Author of life in the stable at Bethlehem, since standing at the foot of the cross, her heart pierced with a sword of sorrow, she saw her Son and her God die, the race of Christian women is endowed with supernatural virtues, and the daughters of Mary have imbibed from their mother a celestial resemblance. The designs of God, which are immutable, have received in them, as it were, a divine prolongation, and they have continued in the Church the rôle of its Mother and Queen of the Church. Whilst the spiritual sovereignty and eternal priesthood of our Lord Jesus Christ are perpetuated in the popes, bishops, and priests, the maternity of Mary, her humility, chastity, and participation in all the mysteries of Christ from Nazareth and Bethlehem unto Calvary, are perpetuated in Christian women; and as this incomparable Virgin brought forth sanctity itself, they give birth to saints by an act at once material and spiritual. In the same way as the Blessed Virgin consented and assisted at the immolation of her Divine Son, as she had consented to the Incarnation, so Christian mothers receive the mission and the race to consent to and assist at the sacrifice of their children immolated for the love of Jesus Christ; and it is a mission and a grace to which they have never been wanting.

I do not know what woman of mind it was that said, in speaking of the sacrifice of Abraham: "God would never have asked this sacrifice of a mother." This poor clever woman, whoever she was, must certainly have never read either the Passion of Jesus Christ or the history of the Church, as she would have undoubtedly seen there that God asked the sacrifice of Abraham of the Virgin Mary, and after her, of thousands of Christian mothers, with this difference, that He has allowed it to be consummated.

This sacrifice, it is true, is beyond the endurance of human strength, but what is impossible to nature is possible and even easy with the supernatural grace of God. The history of the Church is a splendid proof of this truth; and during the persecutions the mothers of the martyrs showed themselves worthy of her whom the Church styles the Queen of Martyrs. At one time it is St. Felicita, a widow and mother of seven sons, like the mother of the Maccabees, whom the Prefect of Rome tries to win by flattery, or to frighten by threats, begging her to spare her children and sacrifice to the idols; but she, instead of yielding, turns towards her sons and says to them: "Look up to heaven, my children; see Jesus Christ awaiting you there with His saints! Remain faithful in his love and save your souls." The Prefect gives her a blow, saying:

"Darest thou speak thus in my presence." Then he called successively the seven young men, who all confessed courageously the name of Jesus Christ. They were all put to death in presence of their mother, who died last in the joy and love of her God. It was the same with Saint Symphrosa, and with the mother of St. Symphorian of Autun and a host of others.

At another time it was St. Yulietta, descendant of a royal race, who was arrested in the city of Tarsus, and brought before Alexander, governor of that city, holding in her arms her infant son, aged three years, and who to all the questions of the pagan, replied: "I am a Christian." The governor took the child away from her, placed him on his knee, and in order to torture the generous Christian more caressed him and tried to prevent his crying; but the poor little child, his eyes fixed on his mother, worked with his little hands and feet to get away from him, and repeated, like his mother:

"I am a Christian! I am a Christian." Alexander, wearied with his cries, seized him by the feet and dashed him to the earth from the height on which he sat. The child's head was broken by the fall, his brains were scattered about, and the earth watered with his blood. His mother seeing this, raised her eyes to heaven and said:

"I thank Thee, Lord, because Thou hast willed that my son should receive before me the immortal crown!" Then she presented her head to the executioner and died, saying: "I long to rejoin my son in the kingdom of heaven."

Later, as time rolls on, the history of the Church is replete with similar traits. When the mother of Blessed John Britto, Jesuit and Missioner in the Indies, heard of the martyrdom of her son, she clothed herself in festive attire, which she had not worn for years, and, giving thanks to God, hastened to Lisbon, whither the king had invited her to receive the congratulations of that pious monarch and his court.

In own days, when the mother of M. Jaccard, a French Missioner, martyred at Tonquin, the 28th of July, 1836, received the fatal yet glorious news, she cried, in the delight of sublime faith: "Thank God! I am delivered from the fear I experienced that he might one day yield to temptation."

Perpetual and admirable unity not only of faith but of Christian heroism at all times and amongst all nations! Listen to what happened during the last bloody persecution at Cochin China. A native Christian was arrested and finally condemned to die for the faith. His mother, hearing of the day of his execution, accompanied him to the block, encouraging him to suffer and die for Jesus Christ. When the head of the martyr was severed from the body she reverently picked it up, and, piously kissing it, enveloped it in her garments, and retired, charged with her precious relic before the eyes of the mandarins and soldiers, who were struck dumb with astonishment. Such have been the Christian mothers in all ages and of all nations, and the mothers of our amiable martyrs of Castelfidardo have proved themselves worthy of their predecessors, and continued this glorious tradition. The letters written by them before and after the sacrifice prove it in an admirable and touching manner. I could have cited these testimonies of truly heroic virtue in relating the history of their children; but each time the name of the son pointed to that of the mother, and I would have wounded the pious susceptibilities of a humility which shuns all show and fears praise.

Christian women wish to be sublime, but on condition that no one knows anything of it. On the contrary, in quoting here a few of these letters, I do not betray any *incognito,* nor wound the holy modesty of those who have written them, and thus the edification of the reader will be satisfied, and the while humility will not lose any of its rights.

First, we have a letter written before the battle of Castelfidardo by the mother of one of the volunteers, who was to die there, and which is, I believe, addressed to the mother of another soldier of the Church:

"It is true, madam, the sacrifice we have made in parting with our children is a great one. But are they not deposits entrusted to our care by God until He asks for them again; and do not Christian mothers see that the moment has come for offering to God that which is dearest to them? When the Church is attacked and needs defenders, is not around the Pontifical throne the place for Catholic young men? And if unfortunately their number is small it is owing to that indifference which has corrupted their hearts. Notwithstanding my grief and anxiety at being separated from my boy, I thank God for having inspired him with such noble sentiments, and preserved him from the general egotism which now prevails. He has never given me aught but pleasure; and, if God spares him he will be a prop to me and his sisters. But, madam, we ought to raise our thoughts on high, and as my dear child said to me in one of his letters: 'If I never see France again it will be for my greater good!' I ought not then to complain of seeing him encounter danger. My son went to Rome, actuated by such pure motives, his aim being to work for the glory of God, that, great as is the sacrifice I have made, I trust Divine Providence will preserve him from those spiritual dangers which parents have more to fear than corporal ones."

God did preserve the soul of the young soldier from those dangers which his mother dreaded more than death. He did more than preserve this soul: He took it to Himself and crowned him with glory, for the son of this admirable Christian mother was one of those who died on the battlefield of Castelfidardo. We have just seen a sacrifice accepted beforehand.

Now we shall see a mother writing to the person who announced to her the death of her son: "I thank God with all my heart for the graces He has bestowed on my son. We shall miss him in our home circle; but for my part, notwithstanding the happiness I would feel in embracing him, I would not recall him to earth. I consider him too happy. If you have encouraged my son in his generous resolution do not think I am annoyed with you. God willed it so. We have, I hope, a powerful intercessor in heaven."

"I feel certain," writes another of these heroic women, "that you will pardon my delay in answering your letter, and that you will ask God to sustain us in the trial He has sent us; for no matter what our consolations may be, consolations for which we can never bless and thank Him sufficiently, there are times when I am quite overcome. I could never dream of asking for my poor child a glory and happiness equal to that which God in His Divine mercy has called him to! More fortunate than many other mothers from whom God asked the same sacrifice, I had the happiness of seeing and nursing my dear child, and of witnessing the many graces which He bestowed on him. You are right, we are happy parents, and in spite of the grief which rends our hearts, we are compelled to rejoice and glorify God for all these graces He has given our dear children. But these graces are so many engagements and obligations for those still on earth, and I ask God, from the depth of my heart, through the intercession of Our Blessed Mother, and our dear children, to grant us grace to correspond with fidelity to all His designs in our regard. We are very grateful, and deeply moved at the souvenir which the Holy Father in his paternal kindness has sent us, and it will be a dear and precious heirloom in our family. We are also deeply grateful for the kind sympathy you have tendered us in our painful yet consoling affliction. Apart from your affectionate sentiments towards us, we like to see in your deeply Catholic sentiments a protestation against those impieties which are so audaciously committed. Let us hope that the blood of those victims, whom God seems to have chosen and marked out, will bear fruit, and open the eyes of those who allow themselves to be seduced."

As I must limit myself, I shall only give one extract more, coming also from a mother heartbroken with grief, but at the same time perfumed by celestial consolations:

"I miss my poor child greatly and feel his loss keenly. The account of his death is most consoling. Here is a passage from a letter which M. Romiti, Canon of Asimo, who was greatly attached to him, wrote to his brother: 'My only aim in attending him was to acquit myself of a very pleasing duty, that of encouraging in his last moments a martyr of Holy Church: it is true my noble friend had no need of me. Oh, how dear is his memory to me! What a glory for your family to count amongst its members a hero and a martyr to so holy a cause. Let your mother find strength and resignation in the consoling thought that she will one day meet her son in heaven with his wounds resplendent with rays of glory.' The prayers of many pious souls have undoubtedly aided our young men; but I have no hesitation in saying that they are indebted for the abundance of their graces and favors to the Mother of God, as they have followed and wished to defend her Son in the person of His Vicar. They have tried to wipe His face, covered with opprobrium: He has not given them his effigy, as He did to St. Veronica; but He has given to them to have part in his wounds. As I have faith in the protection of my son, his love for his nephews and nieces will induce him to help them in the trials of this life, and he will aid me to die well."

We can judge by these few extracts what a fund of faith, resignation, and other heroic virtues filled the souls of these admirable Christians. These letters prove that if the race of the Maccabees is not yet extinct in the Church, or in Catholic

France, neither is the race of the mother of the Maccabees extinct. Yes, the mothers of our martyrs at Castelfidardo resemble that illustrious woman by their heroism and invincible constancy. What do I say? They have even a celestial resemblance to the Mother of God. They are worthy daughters of the Mother of Sorrows, the Queen of Martyrs, and, like this august Virgin, they have stood beneath the cross on which their sons died: *Juxta crucem Jesu stabat mater ejus!* (Next to the cross of Jesus stood his mother!) Before such devotedness and sublime abnegation our Holy Father, the meek and gentle Pius IX, let fall tears from his eyes, and from his lips words of admiration, and uttered, in presence of General de la Moricière, this eulogy, which I repeat with a deep feeling of consolation and hope:

"What souls! What Christians! No; France will not perish! It would be impossible that the Catholic faith should be extinguished in a nation which produces such saints!"

O noble women! real mothers of martyrs! Not alone with feelings of admiration and respect, but with deep gratitude, we ought to salute and bless you, for you are very powerful with God; and Pius IX has said that by the sacrifice of your children, by the blood which they and you have so magnanimously offered, by your prayers, tears, and virtues, you are the true protectresses, the hope, and salvation of France.

CHAPTER XIII

CONCLUSION

I AM NOW AT THE END OF THE PAINFUL, yet consoling task which I proposed to myself: I have ended the history of the Martyrs of Castelfidardo. Since then events have gone on, and rushed down headlong before our eyes with frightful rapidity. Protected by selfish policy, and by the anti-Catholic and anti-French passions of England the revolution daily increased in power, audacity, and impiety. All the Legations, Naples, Sicily, have fallen under its yoke; the King of Naples has only Gaeta; the Pope has only Rome; and if Garibaldi seems to be conquered, his pretended conqueror, Victor Emmanuel, is condemned, under pain of forfeiture, to continue and finish his work of spoliation and ruin. In the meantime, the Piedmontese, besieged, plundered, and robbed the goods of the Church, robbed the people of their rights, and stole millions from the public treasury; shot as insurgents all those who remained faithful to their lawful sovereign, and inaugurated the reign of liberty in Italy by fire, iron, and blood. The bishops were obliged to flee; priests were thrown into prison; religious houses destroyed; immoral writings covered the country like a swarm of noxious insects; theaters resembled places of debauchery; the good trembled, and the wicked triumphed; in a word, the revolution showed more and more its hideousness, and sped on its way with an audacity and insolence, which gave it the assurance of success. Its end it has been said, and repeated daily with an ever-increasing bare-faced effrontery, is nothing less than the overthrow of the Papacy, and the destruction of the Catholic Church. It not alone said it, but it realized it by its acts, and wherever it was mistress it manifested it from time to time by scenes of impiety, the bare mention of which fills the heart with indignation and disgust. I shall only give one example, by quoting a letter from Mgr. Oberson, chaplain to the Swiss Zouaves, who was taken prisoner at Castelfidardo, and shut

up in the fortress of Alexandria. It was from this prison that
he assisted, on the 16th of October, at the diabolical spectacle which he relates:

> "The day passed quietly, but it was only the calm
> preceding the storm. At ten o'clock I was a prey to
> strange forebodings, when suddenly I heard loud cries
> which I could not at first distinguish, then a crowd
> repeated sometimes: 'Ora pro nobis and at other times,
> 'Libera nos Domine,' 'Deliver us, O Lord.' I ran to the
> window, and saw coming out of St. Michael's quar-
> ter, right opposite my cell, a long procession of reli-
> gious, each holding a lighted taper. Two tambourines,
> beating a march, headed the procession as at Rome,
> then came a Capuchin bearing a large cross, followed
> by some hundreds of religious, after these came reli-
> gious of every order in the strangest costumes, then
> the prelates, bishops, cardinals with miters, the guards,
> and lastly the Pope on his throne. At first, on see-
> ing the Capuchins preceded by the cross, and hear-
> ing them chanting the Ora pro nobis, I thought it was
> the funeral of some distinguished officer; but when I
> saw all the miters, and heard the hideous cries of a
> licentious mob, in the middle of the night by the light
> of five or six hundred torches, I no longer doubted
> that it was a horrible profanation. They were about
> to bury the Pope, for they knew well that it was more
> than enough to be faithful to him. I felt myself cov-
> ered with a cold perspiration; my knees bent under
> me. I thought I should have fallen, so overpowered
> was I with my grief at seeing a Catholic people aban-
> don themselves to such atrocities. I made an effort to
> know what these unfortunate men were singing. The
> funeral procession wended its way towards the tow-
> ers of the fortress; suddenly they stopped, and one
> of them pronounced a funeral oration, which was
> an issue of the foulest calumnies against the Pope,
> cardinals, bishops, and all the clergy, uttered by a
> fanatic who yelled like one possessed. Whenever he
> said anything worse than usual, he was encouraged by
> cries of 'Bravo! Bravo! Evviva! Evviva!' and clapping of
> hands. The conclusion of it was that the grandest and

holiest work was the destruction of the Pope and all the priesthood, and this GRAND MISSION Providence reserved for Piedmont, Garibaldi, Cavour, Fanti, Cialdini, and the Piedmontese army, which were to install Victor Emmannuel in the Vatican: this was applauded by thousands of BRAVOS and EVVIVAS. Another orator wished to make himself heard, but his weak voice was drowned by the noise. They then came under my window, and I trembled when I saw them closely, for, O God! what horror! The Capuchins were soldiers belonging to the National Guard, their cloaks answering for a habit, over which was a shirt as a surplice, and forming a hood of part of the cloak, they let it fall over the surplice. The bishops and cardinals had large horns coming out at each side of the mitre, as if to signify so many demons; the pope was immovable; he had expired, crushed by the weight of a monstrous tiara. The litanies were:

'St. Garibaldi, Liberator of Italy, pray for us.'

'St. Cavour, who knew how to baffle the intrigues of the Jesuits, pray for us.'

'Sts. Fanti, Cialdini, who didst crush De la Moricière and the infamous army of priests, pray for us.'

All the other saints were of the same character. From time to time they shouted evvivas for brothers and friends. When passing the artillery quarters they sang: 'Long live our artillery brethren, who shot the soldiers of the Pope! Long live the Piedmontese army, always victorious!' Then they invoked some female saint worthy of figuring in the Alexandrine litany, after which was added, 'Holy Liberty, Equality, Fraternity, Republic. May they be extended from pole to pole!' Under my windows they sang:

'From the oppressors of Italy, *Libera nos Domine*; from the Pope and his priesthood, *Libera nos Domine*, Deliver us O Lord!' and several other revolting titles which I would refrain from repeating: '93 never produced anything more hideous, impious, and disgusting. Suddenly there was a great silence: this was the colonel who interfered when all was over, and the scandal finished.'"

Such is the policy of the day. You will ask me, who are these unnatural beings who abandon themselves to such horrible profanations? They are the soldiers of the gallant king. This disgusting scene was organized and directed by a Major of the National Guard, enacted and applauded by the officers and soldiers of the fortress of Alexandria. Such are the troops sent to Rome, to protect the Holy Father, to guard the holy city, and to defend religion. "My God, remember Thy mercies, and give sight to the blind ones of our age." No, never before has impiety in the delirium of its madness produced such foolish ignominies; and, in truth, it seems, when reading of these crimes, that we are lifting a corner of that mysterious veil which hides from our sight the other world, and that we are permitted to see the horrors of hell.

And this is the end, the infernal, avowed end of the Revolution! and it will not stop until it has attained it. What it aims at is the destruction of the Papacy, because it knows that without the Pope there would be no Church, as without the head the human body would have no life; then without the Church, no more Christianity; without Christianity, no more religion; without religion, no more society, but a vile mob, a pallid flock of slaves, bent and brutalized under the bloody yoke of the base Commune.

Such is the end of the Revolution; and yet, strange blindness! notwithstanding the evidence of this, we see a crowd of well-meaning people, even practical Christians, who smile at these Italian events, who blame the Pope and the King of Naples, excuse Victor Emmanuel, almost admire Garibaldi, and assist with secret sympathy at all the triumphs of this frightful power. But if some are blind, there are others who see things clearly, and whose eyes are open to the dangers which surround them. According as the wicked throw off the mask by which they are covered, the good withdraw from them and unite closer to one another, by drawing nearer to the common center of good and truth in this world. The good grain and the tare will be separated, and soon, with the grace of God, illusions will become so manifest that here below there will be but two fields that of the Church and the Revolution. Yes; the storm rumbles in the distance, the sinister creakings are heard on all sides; it seems that a period of universal disorder is approaching. But if there be lives, institutions, societies, which appear tottering to decay and death, others, though seemingly dead, will rise again and live. The old East is struggling with life in its sepulcher, which they believed to be sealed forever. The cross will reappear, free and victorious, in China, thanks to the arms of France, which is always in some manner the soldier of God in the world. Nearer home, in Italy, where at this moment are being discussed the destinies of human consciences and European civilization, devoted characters increase with its iniquities. The Pope is still at Rome, greater and more honored than his triumphant persecutors. From all parts of the world come the generous and ever-increasing offerings of Catholics to the Holy See; the rich give their gold, and the poor their mite. According as the waves of impiety and revolution swell, so also swell the generous love and indignation of Catholics round that bark, always threatened, yet ever subsisting which bears with the successor of Peter the hope and salvation of the world. Bishops, priests, and laity fill the ranks and press around their chief and father, ready to suffer everything for him and with him. They know that the Revolution can have only a short-lived triumph; they know, too, that it can accumulate many ruins, and cause the children of the Church to shed torrents of tears and blood; but they console themselves, and hope and wait with unshaken confidence for the day of reparation, the day of resurrection, the day of Jesus Christ; and whilst their enemies, infatuated by pride and hatred, intone the *De Profundis* of the Church and the Papacy, they meditate in silence on these two grand Gospel sentences, which have never yet deceived them during eighteen hundred years:

"Thou art Peter, and upon this rock I will build my Church, and the gates of hell shall not prevail against it."

"Whoever will fall on this rock will be broken, and he on whom it will fall will be reduced to dust."

Long live Pius IX, our Pontiff King!

Long live the Holy, Roman, Catholic, and Apostolical Church!

Live forever, Jesus Christ, the Word made flesh, sole Master, sole Lord, alone all-powerful with God His Father in the unity of the Holy Ghost!

Amen! Amen!

Amen, in spite of blasphemies and impiety!

Amen, in spite of the fleeting triumph of the Revolution!

Amen, in spite of the efforts of hell!

It is so, and it will be so throughout all ages and for eternity!

Amen!

FIN